C000183077

FAT FREE
Indian
COOKERY

FAT FREE
Indian
COOKERY

**The revolutionary new way
to enjoy healthy and
delicious Indian food**

Mridula Baljekar

metro

Published by Metro Publishing Ltd,
3 Bramber Court, 2 Bramber Road, London W14 9PB, England

This edition first published in paperback in 2002

ISBN 1 84358 001 2

British Library Cataloguing-in-Publication Data: A catalogue record for this
book is available from the British Library.

Photography by Ken Field
Illustrations by Sophie Joyce
Cover design by ENVY
Typeset by SX Composing DTP, Rayleigh, Essex
Printed and bound in Great Britain by CPD (Wales)

3 5 7 9 10 8 6 4 2

Papers used by Metro Publishing Ltd are natural, recyclable products made
from wood grown in sustainable forests. The manufacturing processes conform
to the environmental regulations of the country of origin.

CONTENTS

This book is dedicated to all those who believe that healthy eating is a way of life and that NO FAT does not necessarily mean NO TASTE.

ACKNOWLEDGEMENTS

I am grateful to:

Reader's Digest for their fascinating book entitled *Foods That Harm Foods That Heal* which helped me to discover the benefits of many ingredients used in this book.

To K. T. Achaya for his excellent book *Indian Food – A Historical Companion.*

To Magimix for supplying gadgets.

To Total Greek Yogurt Company for supplying samples.

To the Solo Sea Salt Company for sending samples which made me realize that low-sodium salt does not impair flavours.

To my daughter, Maneesha, for her help in proofreading.

INTRODUCTION

When you think of Indian food do you have visions of meat and vegetables floating in a sea of oil? Do you sometimes wish it wasn't so oily and that you could eat it more often? Now there is a way.

My revolutionary cooking method will give you the chance to enjoy delicious Indian meals, packed with flavour, health and vitality, but without significant quantities of added fat!

The majority of the recipes have the right type of fat in minimum quantities and in many cases oil is not added at all. These unique dishes will not only give you great taste but also guard your health.

I am not suggesting that you exclude fat altogether from your diet. Indeed, some fat is essential to the body. Fat enhances the flavour of any food, not just Indian food. Fat is also an important nutrient and a high source of energy. It is also a carrier of fat-soluble vitamins. Fats and oils help enhance the characteristic aroma, taste and texture of most food. It is knowing which type of fat to include and which to avoid, or consume in small quantities, that is the first and most important step in following a healthy diet.

There are three crucial types of fats that affect our diet. These are:

Saturates (present mainly in animal fats, but also in coconut and palm oil);

Mono-unsaturates (found mainly in olive oil, also in rapeseed oil, nut and seed oils);

Polyunsaturates (found in vegetable, nut and seed oils, as well as oily fish such as mackerel, sardines, salmon and herrings).

According to guidelines set out by the Health Education Authority, saturated fat is not really needed in our diet. High intake of this fat can create high blood cholesterol which can lead to heart diseases and cancer. Reducing saturates in our diet is essential to maintain a healthy lifestyle.

By reducing or avoiding saturates, we automatically reduce the energy supply to our body. This gap can be closed by using more of the two beneficial types of fats: mono-unsaturates and poly-unsaturates (omega-3 fatty acids), which are believed to be beneficial to the heart.

In Indian cooking, oil or ghee is used to fry onions and spices. I must admit that, very often, a lot more is used than is actually necessary. Frying the spices before adding the main ingredient is the very essence of Indian cooking. Spices need to be fried gently to enhance their flavours and achieve the desired taste and texture. But it is not always necessary to fry the spices in oil or ghee. Nor is it necessary to do this at the beginning of the cooking process. This can also be done *without any added fat in the middle or at the end of the process.*

INVISIBLE FAT

Everyone is aware of 'invisible fat', i.e. the fat that is naturally present in certain types of food. One day, during a frantic rush to get the family meal ready, I discovered that I could use this natural fat to fry the spices and produce delicious Indian dishes without any added fat. The fact that I simply had to use up some marinated lamb, which had sat in my fridge for 36 hours, led to this discovery. I put the lamb in a heavy saucepan and just let it stew in its own juices until it was almost tender. I then dried off all the natural juices by leaving the pan uncovered and, when it was completely dry, I browned the meat in its own fat, cooking the spices at the same time! A hint of coconut milk (it is very high in fat, so only a dash) and fresh coriander to finish off the dish produced one of the most delicious lamb curries I had ever tasted, and my family agreed.

In my excitement, I embarked on a long process of testing Indian recipes using the minimum of fat and this book is the result.

I always loved watching my mother and grandmother creating wonderful-looking and delicious dishes. Once, when I was about 10 years old, I remember my mother telling me that what the spices really needed to enhance their flavours was *heat*. Gentle heat activates the volatile oils in the spices and greatly enhances their flavour. The important factor is the correct level of heat. Too much heat will dry out the essential oils and ruin the flavour; too little will do nothing to enhance them. This made more sense to me when, later on, I saw how my mother-in-law gently roasted the whole spices before grinding them. She added the roasted and ground spices to her chosen dish without frying them again. She would then add a hot oil seasoning to finish the dish.

The process of dry-roasting the spices is quite quick and simple. These dishes were very low in fat as they consisted mainly of vegetables, pulses and beans. In most of my recipes I have used this technique, but omitted the hot oil seasoning in the meat and poultry dishes. There is enough natural fat in meat and poultry. The dishes turned out very well. This further convinced me that adding extra fat was quite unnecessary.

The absence of natural fat, however, makes it difficult to cook vege-tables, lentils, beans and certain types of fish without sacrificing the flavour. To overcome this, I have used small quantities of polyunsaturated fat, such as sunflower or soya oil, in all these recipes.

With a little care and imagination, and a lot of patience, I have achieved authentic flavours in both newly created and traditional recipes. Indian food is generally very healthy because of the generous use of fresh vege-tables, beans, pulses and wholewheat flour for the everyday bread (chapatis). Combine this with meat, fish and poultry dishes with no added fat and you have a winning formula for a healthy lifestyle.

There is one important point which I would like you to remember when using this book: by added fat I mean mainly *saturated fat*. Certain types of fat are actually beneficial to our health. I have not excluded the following items as they are perfectly safe as long as we consume them in moderation.

Nuts: All types of nuts are good sources of protein and vitamin E. They are also a high source of fat, but it is a 'good' fat, so can be used in small quantities.

Seeds: Sesame and poppy seeds are also high in fat but only small quantities are required. They are great flavour enhancers and are an essential part of Indian cooking. They help thicken the sauces too. Sunflower seeds are a good source of fibre and lend a wonderfully nutty taste to a sauce, thickening it at the same time.

Dairy Products: Reduced-fat alternatives such as skimmed or semi-skimmed milk, low-fat natural yogurt, Greek yogurt, cream substitutes, (these are sold under the Elmlea and Delight brand names and are made of vegetable oil and buttermilk), fromage frais, half-fat crème fraîche and paneer (Indian cheese) are all acceptable in small quantities.

Coconut: This has a high fat content, so I have used it sparingly in a few recipes for the sake of taste and authentic flavour. I have avoided creamed coconut except for one recipe (see Lamb in Coconut Milk, page 108). This was my first prototype recipe which launched the whole concept of cooking Indian food without added fat.

MY METHODS FOR GREAT FLAVOURS

1. Pre-cooked onion purée is used as fat is required to fry onion. As spring onions can be used raw, and fried in much less oil than ordinary onions, I have used them in many recipes with great success.
2. Pre-roasted ground spices are used in the majority of the recipes, this adds loads of flavour, but no fat.
3. Tandoori dishes are low fat in any case, but I have further reduced the fat by not using oil or butter for basting, as is usually done. They taste delicious with my fat-free basting sauces.
4. Traditional deep-fried dishes have been adapted for grilling or baking with a light brushing of oil for fabulous results.

SOME HINTS

There are a few important points to remember before you embark on this revolutionary cooking method:

1. You do need to invest in a couple of good-quality non-stick saucepans. A non-stick surface is safer for this method of cooking, as you will be able to cook the spices without them sticking to the pan. When the spices stick to the pan, they can burn quickly, spoiling the flavour completely. A non-stick pan also allows you to use as little oil as possible.
2. As oil-free cooking is designed for a healthy lifestyle, it is also a good idea to choose the food you want to cook with care. The following items are listed in ascending order of fat content:

* Fish (1% in general. Oily fish like mackerel has more of the poly-unsaturates, which are beneficial)
* Skinned chicken breast (4% fat)
* Pork (4% fat)
* Beef (4.6% fat)
* Lamb (8.8% fat)

3. In Indian dishes, poultry is always skinned, and excess fat removed from meat and poultry, before cooking. This method is even more important in fat-free cooking. Always remove the skin from chicken as this is the highest source of fat. Also remove as much visible fat as you can from all meat and poultry. You will still find just enough fat oozing out of them to fry the spices.

ABOUT SALT

In Indian cooking, salt plays an important part in achieving a balanced flavour with the spices. The important points to consider are the type of food to which the salt is added and whether extra salt is to be added to the dish at the table.

Only raw fish, poultry and meat, which have no added salt (unlike ham or bacon), are used in Indian cooking. As we achieve a well-rounded flavour with the right amount of spices and salt during cooking, adding salt at the dining table has rarely been a part of an Indian meal. Instead of stock cubes, Indian cooking makes use of home-made, highly aromatic stocks with no added salt.

In all the recipes, I have used the right amount of salt needed to create a balanced flavour. If the level of salt still seems high to you compared to Western cooking, and if it is enough to worry you, then by all means adjust it to your liking. It is the sodium that causes the problem. There are low-sodium versions of salt available in most supermarkets. You could use one of these as an alternative.

WEIGHT LOSS AND HEALTHY EATING
Although you will certainly benefit from a low-fat diet, I do not claim that this book is the answer to a slimmer's dream. By ensuring that no added fat is used in the recipes, you have taken the first and foremost step to following a healthy diet. Neither is this book a manual for healthy eating, but you can safely use it as a guide. To help you, each recipe is accompanied by a nutritional analysis telling you how many calories (Kcals), how many grams of fat (g fat) and how many grams of saturated fat (g saturated fat) each serving contains. (The saturated fat is part of the total amount of fat, not in addition to it.) Where a recipe provides a range of portions (for example, serves 4–5), the analysis is for the smaller number of portions (that is, in this example, 4, not 5).

My aim is to give you the chance to enjoy Indian food without having to worry about consuming too much fat. Sensible control of calories is essential to keep well. Fat contains more calories per gram than any other food group. Cutting down on fat, therefore, must top the list of priorities in formulating a healthy eating routine. If fat that is naturally present in food is enough to enhance the flavours of spices, why add more?

Remember, risk follows fat. This book offers you no added fat, no risk and great taste!

Happy cooking! Eat well! Live well!

A GUIDE TO INGREDIENTS

The following is a list of some of the ingredients used in this book. If you are unsure about how to buy and store certain ingredients, this list, together with the Cook's Tips included throughout, should help.

ANISEED (ajowain or carum)
Anise is native to India. This resembles a celery seed and is related to caraway and cumin, though the flavour is more akin to thyme. All Indian grocers sell anise and the seeds will keep for a number of years if stored in an airtight container. They are used with pulses and fried snacks. Anise aids digestion and helps to prevent wind.

CHAPATI FLOUR (atta)
Very fine wholewheat flour used to make all unleavened Indian bread. This is rich in dietary fibre because, unlike wholemeal flour, atta is made by grinding the whole grain to a very fine powder.

BAY LEAF (tej patta)
Bay leaves used in Indian cooking are obtained from the cassia tree and are quite different from Western bay leaves (from the sweet bay laurel). As Indian bay leaves are not easily available, standard bay leaves can be used instead.

BLACK PEPPERCORNS (kali mirchi)
Fresh green berries are dried in the sun to obtain black pepper. The green berries come from the pepper vine native to monsoon forests of south-west India. Whole peppercorns will keep well in an airtight jar but ground black pepper loses its wonderful aromatic flavour very quickly. It is best to keep a supply of whole pepper in a mill and grind it only when required. Pepper is believed to be a good remedy for flatulence.

CARDAMOM (elaichi)
Cardamom has been used in Indian cooking since ancient times. Southern India produces an abundance of cardamom and it is from there that this spice found its way to Europe via the ancient spice route.
      There are two types of cardamom. The small green cardamoms (*choti elaichi*) and the big dark brown cardamoms, which are generally referred to as black cardamoms. In the West, we also see a third variety, white cardamoms, which are obtained by blanching small green cardamoms. This produces a milder flavour.
      Whole green cardamom pods are used to flavour rice and different sauces. Ground cardamom, used in many desserts and drinks, can be bought from Indian stores. However, it is best to grind small quantities at home using a coffee or spice mill. If stored for too long, the essential natural oils will dry out which destroys the flavour.
      In India, cardamom seeds are chewed after a meal as a mouth freshener.

CHILLIES (mirchi)

It is difficult to judge the strength of chillies. Generally, the small, thin chillies are hot and the large fleshy ones tend to be milder. Most of the heat comes from the seeds, so it is best to remove them if you do not enjoy hot food. You can do this by halving the chillies lengthways, then scraping out the seeds under running water using a small knife. The other method is to roll the chillies between the palms of your hands for a few seconds. This loosens the seeds, then you can slit the chilli without cutting it through completely and shake out the seeds.

Always wash your hands thoroughly after handling chillies as their juices are a severe irritant, particularly to eyes or tender areas of skin. To remove all traces of pungency, rub a little oil into your hands, then rub in lemon juice.

Fresh green chillies: Long, slim fresh green chillies are sold in Indian stores. Chillies that come from the Canary Islands tend to be milder than Indian chillies. Jalapeño and serrano chillies from Mexico are more readily available in supermarkets – they are not ideal for Indian cooking, but they can be used.

Fresh red chillies: Mainly from Thailand, these are sold in most large supermarkets.

Dried red chillies (lal mirchi): When fresh green chillies are ripe, they turn a rich red. These are dried to produce dried red chillies, which have a completely different flavour. Fresh chillies cannot be used instead of dried (nor dried for fresh). Crushed dried chillies are coarsely ground. They are sold in Indian and Pakistani shops or they can be prepared at home in a coffee or spice mill. Supermarkets also sell crushed dried red chillies. Dried chillies are ground into chilli powder.

Bird's eye chillies: Small, pointed and extremely hot, these are normally used whole to flavour oil. Long slim chillies are weaker and they are ground with other spices.

CINNAMON

One of the oldest spices, cinnamon is obtained from the dried bark of a tropical plant related to the laurel family. It has a warm flavour valued in savoury and sweet dishes.

CLOVES (lavang)

These are the unripened buds of a South-Asian evergreen tree. They have a distinctive flavour and are used both whole and ground. In India, cloves are used as a breath freshener. Clove oil is used to ease toothache.

COCONUT (nariyal)

Coconut palms grow in abundance in southern India and fresh coconut is used in savoury and sweet dishes. Alternatives to fresh coconut include desiccated and creamed coconut. Coconut milk powder is available in an instant form. Canned coconut milk is also available. Use unsweetened desiccated coconut (it is usually unsweetened, but there are some sweet, long-thread, dried coconut products) and check that canned coconut milk is unsweetened if you use that. Coconut has a high saturated fat content.

CORIANDER SEEDS (dhaniya)
The seeds from the plant which provides fresh leaves used as a herb, this is one of the most important spices in Indian cooking. Its sweet, mellow flavour blends well with vegetables.

CORIANDER, FRESH (hara dhaniya)
The fresh leaves of the coriander plant, this herb is widely used in Indian cooking for flavour as well as to garnish food. This is also the basis for many chutneys and pastes.

CUMIN (jeera)
This pungent spice can be used whole or ground and the quantity should always be measured as the flavour is strong. The seeds are used whole to flavour oil before vegetables are added. A more rounded flavour is obtained if the seeds are roasted, then ground.

There are two varieties, black (*kala jeera*) and white (*safed jeera*), each with its own distinctive flavour. The two are not interchangeable. Black cumin is sometimes confused with caraway.

CURRY LEAVES (kari patta)
Grown and used extensively all over southern India, these have an assertive flavour. They are used with vegetables and pulses. They are sold fresh or dried in Indian grocers' shops. The dried leaves can be stored in an airtight jar and the fresh ones (which have a better flavour) can be frozen, then added to dishes when required.

FENNEL (saunf)
These green-yellow seeds are slightly larger than cumin and they have a flavour similar to anise. They have been used in Indian cooking since ancient times and they are also chewed as a breath freshener or to settle an upset stomach.

GARAM MASALA (see page 22)
Garam means heat and *masala* is the blending of different spices. The main ingredients in this spice mix are cinnamon or cassia, cloves and black pepper, with other spices according to individual taste. These main ingredients are believed to create body heat and they are used to make a warming spiced tea in extreme climates in the Himalayan region.

GARLIC (lasoon)
Fresh garlic is indispensable in Indian cooking. Dried flakes, powder and garlic salt cannot give the same authentic flavour. It is always used crushed or puréed to yield the maximum flavour. Garlic is believed to be beneficial in reducing blood cholesterol levels; it also has antiseptic properties and aids digestion.

GINGER (adrak)
Fresh root ginger is vital to Indian cooking, with its fresh, but warm and

woody flavour. Dried (powdered) ginger cannot give the same fresh flavour. Ginger is believed to reduce acidity in the stomach and promote good blood circulation.

GRAM FLOUR OR CHICK-PEA FLOUR (besan)
Made from ground chick peas, this is available from Indian shops.

MINT (pudina)
Native to the Mediterranean and West-Asian countries, mint is easy to grow and readily available. Dried mint is a good substitute in Indian cooking.

MOONG DHAL
From Indian shops, these are skinned and split mung beans.

MUSTARD (sarsoon or rai)
Mustard seeds are essential in Indian vegetarian cooking. Black and brown seeds are most commonly used and white seeds are reserved for pickles. Black and brown seeds have a nutty flavour. Mustard leaves are used as a vegetable.

NUTMEG (jaiphal)
Nutmeg has a hard dark-brown shell with a lacy covering. This covering is mace, the highly aromatic and brightly coloured spice, which is removed from the nutmeg before the latter is sold. Buy whole nutmegs as the ready ground spice loses its lovely aroma and flavour quickly. Use a small nutmeg grater for grating the whole nut.

ONION SEEDS (kalonji)
These tiny black seeds are not true onion seeds, they have been given this name only because they bear a striking resemblance to onion seeds. These are used whole for flavouring fish, vegetables, pickles and breads.

PANEER: Often referred to as cottage cheese in Indian, this is quite different from Western cottage cheese. Ricotta resembles paneer in flavour, but not in appearance, texture or cooking qualities. Paneer is a firm, unripened and unsalted cheese which does not melt and run like other cheeses when cooked, but withstands high temperatures to retain its shape. Paneer is available from larger supermarkets (sold pre-packed). Halloumi is the nearest Western cheese I have found but it is salted, so salt quantities in recipes have to be adjusted when it is used instead of paneer.

PAPRIKA
Hungary and Spain produce mild, sweet peppers that are dried and ground to make paprika. Deghi Mirchi is grown extensively in Kashmir as the main plant for making Indian paprika which is mild, and it tints dishes with a brilliant red without making them hot to eat.

POPPY SEEDS (khus khus)
The opium poppy produces the best seeds. There are two varieties, black or

white, and only the white are used in Indian cooking. They are ground (sometimes roasted) and contribute a nutty flavour to sauces as well as acting as a thickening agent.

RED LENTILS (Masoor dhal)
These can be bought from Indian grocers or from supermarkets.

ROSE WATER
The essence of an edible rose, the petals of which are used to garnish Mogul dishes, diluted for use in savoury and sweet dishes.

ROSE-FLAVOURED SYRUP (rooh afza)
This is available from Indian shops. Rose water can be used instead, but the flavour is less concentrated and it is not sweetened.

ROYAL CUMIN (shahi jeera)
Different from standard cumin, this rare, more expensive, variety grows mainly in Kashmir. It has a delicate, yet distinctive, flavour. The seeds will keep almost indefinitely if stored in an airtight jar.

SAFFRON (kesar)
The saffron crocus grows extensively in Kashmir and some 250,000 stamens are required to produce just 500g of saffron. Only a minute quantity of this expensive, concentrated spice is required to flavour a dish.

SESAME SEEDS (til)
Pale, creamy seeds with a rich nutty flavour. They are indigenous to India, which is the largest exporter of sesame oil to the West. Sprinkled on naan before baking, the seeds are also used with vegetables and in some sweet dishes. They are also used to thicken sauces.

TAMARIND (imli)
Resembling pea pods at first, tamarind pods turn dark brown with a thin outer shell when ripe. The chocolate-brown flesh is encased in the shell, with seeds which have to be removed. The flesh is soaked in hot water to yield a pulp. Ready-to-use concentrated tamarind pulp is quick and easy to use. Valued for its distinctive tangy flavour, tamarind is added to vegetables, lentils and other pulses, and chutneys.

TOOR DHAL
These are yellow split lentils. They are available from Indian shops.

TURMERIC (haldi)
Fresh turmeric rhizomes resemble small pieces of ginger, with a beige-brown skin and bright yellow flesh. Fresh turmeric is dried and ground to produce the familiar spice, which has to be measured carefully to avoid giving dishes a bitter taste.

WHOLEWHEAT CHAPATI FLOUR (atta)
Available from Indian shops, this can be stored in the same way as ordinary flour. A combination of wholemeal and white flour can be substituted (half and half) if this is not available.

YELLOW SPLIT PEAS (channa dhal)
From supermarkets or in large bags from Indian shops.

YOGURT (dahi)
In India yogurt is always home-made, usually from buffalo milk which is creamier than cow's milk. Indian yogurt is mild. Throughout the recipes, low-fat plain yogurt is listed and I recommend using bio or live yogurt with a mild taste as it matches Indian yogurt better than ordinary types.

A WELL-STOCKED STORECUPBOARD

Indian cooking is enjoyable when you have a well-stocked storecupboard. It is worth making a trip to a good Indian shop to stock up on ingredients that are more economical from specialist outlets. These are ingredients I always keep in stock.

SPICES
Keep a supply of all the spices and seeds already listed, storing them in airtight jars, away from direct light. As well as whole spices, have the following ground spices: coriander, chilli powder, cumin, garam masala (bought or home-made, see page 22), paprika and turmeric. Curry leaves and bay leaves can be dried or the fresh leaves can be frozen.

DRY INGREDIENTS
Apart from the usual dry ingredients readily available from all supermarkets, dhal, besan (gram or chick-pea flour) and chapati flour are useful for Indian cooking. Basmati rice is, of course, essential.

CANNED FOOD
Chopped tomatoes are fairly standard storecupboard items, and pulses are versatile: chick peas, butter beans and kidney beans are used in this book. Although not a canned food, tomato purée is another item to keep in stock (a tube is more convenient than a can).

STANDARD FRESH INGREDIENTS
Onions are, of course, essential in every kitchen for the majority of savoury cooking. Garlic, root ginger and chillies are also essential for Indian cooking. Store garlic and ginger in a cool dry place, preferably with potatoes. Remove the stalks from fresh green chillies, then store them in an airtight jar in the refrigerator for 3–4 weeks. They can also be frozen. Onion, garlic and ginger can also be made into purées and chilled or frozen (see

Basic Recipes).

Coriander leaves bought in a bunch with roots intact can be stored in a jug of water for 6–7 days (change the water daily). Alternatively, wrap the roots with damp kitchen paper and tie the bunch in a large polythene bag, then store in the salad drawer of the refrigerator. Tie the bag loosely, excluding air, and store it with the roots down. Alternatively, chopped coriander freezes well and is ready for immediate use.

SPECIALIST ITEMS
Tamarind concentrate or juice and rose-flavoured syrup (*rooh afza*) are useful. Coconut milk powder is available from larger supermarkets and it is convenient particularly because it has a long shelf life and it can be used in small quantities. Unlike desiccated coconut, coconut milk powder does not have to be ground or soaked and strained.

Basic
Recipes

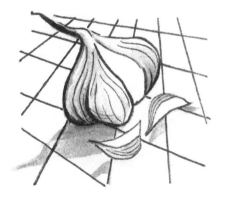

Fat makes food tasty – that's why we like it so much. These basic preparations replace and enhance flavours which may be diminished by reducing or omitting fat from recipes. They also make Indian cooking simpler and speedier. Many of the items in this chapter can be bought prepared, but the home-made version is vastly superior in flavour and aroma.

In a modern kitchen, a coffee or spice mill, blender and food processor replace the traditional grinding stone. A coffee mill is used to prepare many ingredients in this book and a blender and/or food processor is also used throughout.

ROASTING SPICES

Spices are roasted in a dry pan. A cast-iron or heavy-based frying pan or small saucepan is best. A heavy pan retains heat after the heat source has been turned off and roasts spices evenly. Throughout the recipes, where ingredients are dry roasted, use a heavy-based pan; if you have only thin cookware, take care to regulate the heat otherwise the ingredients burn more easily.

Be sure to roast the spices at the correct temperature and for the times specified. Under- or overcooking the spices will not improve their flavours; in fact, if overcooked, some essential oils in the spices are lost, resulting in less flavour.

Remove the spices from the pan immediately to prevent further cooking, and spread them out on a plate. Leave to cool for about 5 minutes before grinding.

GARLIC PURÉE

MAKES 500g (1lb 2oz)

Preparation time: 30 minutes

Garlic is used in most Indian dishes, except for those cooked on religious occasions. This is because it is considered to be a stimulant, not to be consumed on days when the mind should be void of all temptation. Preparing fresh garlic for each recipe can be time-consuming, but it is easy to make a batch of garlic purée and store it in the refrigerator or freezer. When buying garlic, look for firm, plump and unbroken bulbs. Fresh bulbs, tinged with pink, are juicy, delicious and full of essential oils. Store garlic at room temperature, ideally in a cool, dry place.

8–10 garlic bulbs, about 450g (1lb), peeled

¼ teaspoon citric acid (optional)

- To peel the garlic, first lightly crush the cloves with gentle pressure to loosen the skin. The back of a wooden spoon or a large knife can be used for this. Remove the skins.

- Purée the garlic in a blender with 150ml (5fl oz) water. Store the garlic purée in an airtight container in the refrigerator. It will keep for up to 15 days; it may discolour slightly, but this will not affect the flavour. If you are worried about the garlic discolouring, add the citric acid when puréeing the garlic.

- Freeze garlic purée in small airtight freezer containers, placing them in a sealed polythene bag to prevent the garlic odour from tainting other foods in the freezer. Freeze for up to 6 months.

* COOK'S TIP: When preparing 1–2 garlic cloves for a recipe, it is easier to leave the cloves whole (even though this makes peeling them slightly more difficult) and then either grate them on the fine blade of a grater or crush them with a little salt to make a smooth pulp. For 1 teaspoon smooth purée, use 1 large or 2 medium garlic cloves.

* HEALTHY HINT: In India, garlic has been used for thousands of years to cure ailments such as bronchitis, asthma, colds and coughs. It has also been used in ritual healing. Modern research suggests that garlic may help to lower blood cholesterol and inhibit blood clots.

Basic Recipes 15

GINGER PURÉE

Preparation time: 10–15 minutes

Along with onion and garlic, ginger is one of the three ingredients that make up the well-known 'wet trinity' used in Indian cooking. When buying ginger, look for a piece which feels firm and has thin, shiny skin. Store ginger in a cool, dry place, away from direct light. Unless grated or puréed, ginger does not keep well in the refrigerator. Ideally, store it with potatoes for best results. Prepared ginger sold in jars or tubes does not have the same flavour as this home-made purée.

450g (1lb) fresh root ginger, peeled and coarsely chopped

- Purée the ginger with 150ml (5fl oz) water in a blender until smooth. Mature ginger root is fibrous and requires slightly longer blending than young roots. Continue blending until you achieve a smooth texture.

- Store the ginger purée in an airtight container in the refrigerator. It will keep for up to 15 days. Alternatively, freeze the purée in small, airtight freezer containers. Freeze for up to 6 months.

---

* **COOK'S TIP:** It is easier to use a vegetable peeler than a knife to peel ginger and you do not lose any of the flesh. Instead of puréeing ginger, it can be grated on a fairly fine blade of a grater (but not the finest, as the ginger will stick to it). For 1 teaspoon finely grated ginger, use a 2.5cm (1in) cube of fresh root ginger.

---

* **HEALTHY HINT:** Ginger was used by ancient Chinese and Indian herbalists as a cure for acidity, nausea and poor circulation. Fresh ginger juice mixed with honey is still given as a cure for a dry, tickly cough.

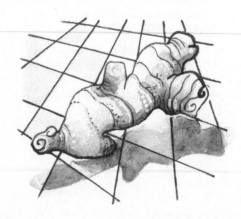

BOILED ONION PURÉE

Preparation time: 10 minutes
Cooking time: 15 minutes

Onions are cooked in different ways to achieve the characteristic textures and flavours of individual dishes. Boiled onion purée is commonly used to thicken sauces, adding its own distinctive flavour when cooked with spices. Even though I have not used large quantities of fat for frying onions and spices in the recipes, I am amazed at the fantastic flavours produced by these traditional ingredients when they are combined with the modest amount of fat naturally present in meat and poultry.

750g (1lb 10oz) onions, coarsely chopped

6 green cardamom pods, bruised

- Place the onions and cardamoms in a saucepan. Pour in 600ml (1 pint) water and bring to the boil. Reduce the heat to medium, cover and cook for 15 minutes, or until the onions are soft. Set aside to cool.

- Remove the cardamom pods and purée the onions with their cooking liquid in a blender. Store in an airtight container in the refrigerator for 8–10 days. Alternatively, pack in 225g (8oz) portions in airtight containers and freeze for up to 6 months.

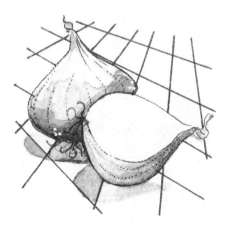

BROWNED SLICED ONIONS

Preparation time: 5 minutes
Cooking time: 10–15 minutes

Fried onions are a popular, appetizing garnish for many Indian dishes, particularly rice dishes, such as pilaus and biryanis. Add a special touch to plain boiled rice by topping it with a little fried onion. Try this low-fat version of fried onions – the quantity given is enough to garnish at least two dishes.

2 large onions, peeled, halved and finely sliced

¼ teaspoon sugar

¾ teaspoon salt

2 teaspoons sunflower or soya oil

- Place the onions in a non-stick frying pan with the remaining ingredients and cook over medium heat for 3–4 minutes.

- Add 3 tablespoons water and continue to cook for a further 3–4 minutes, until the onions begin to brown.

- Pour in 75ml (2½fl oz) water and cook for 4–5 minutes, until the onions are soft and the water has evaporated. Continue to cook for another 1–2 minutes, if necessary, until the onions are well browned. Remove from the heat and use as required. The onions can be stored in a covered container in the refrigerator for 4–5 days.

---

* **COOK'S TIP: A large quantity of onions can be prepared and frozen. Pack them in airtight containers and freeze for up to 6 months.**

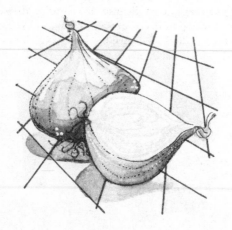

BROWNED ONION PURÉE

Preparation time: 15 minutes
Cooking time: about 30 minutes

In their traditional dishes, north-Indian chefs fry the onions until well browned, then purée them. This creates a wonderful flavour and thickens sauces at the same time. To achieve this without fat, I have browned the onions with a little salt and sugar by cooking them slowly until the sugar caramelizes.

900g (2lb) onions, finely sliced

1 teaspoon salt

1 tablespoon sugar

- Mix the ingredients in a saucepan and stir over low heat. When the onions begin to sizzle, sprinkle in 1 tablespoon water, stir well and cover the pan. Cook for 15 minutes, by which time the onions will have released all their natural moisture.

- Increase the heat to medium and cook, uncovered and stirring frequently, for a further 12–15 minutes or until the liquid has evaporated.

- Remove from the heat and set aside to cool slightly. Process the onions until smooth in a food processor or blender, or press them through a sieve. Use as required.

- The purée can be stored in an airtight container in the refrigerator for up to 15 days. Alternatively, make a large quantity and freeze it in 225g (8oz) batches, which is the average quantity used in a recipe. The purée can be frozen for up to 6 months.

* **HEALTHY HINT: Onions may help to reduce high blood cholesterol and reduce the risk of coronary heart disease. Like garlic, they are believed to contain a compound which helps to prevent the blood from clotting and may increase the rate at which clots are broken down. They also contain sulphur compounds which may help to prevent the growth of cancer cells.**

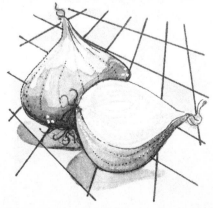

GROUND ROASTED CUMIN

MAKES 225g (8oz)

Preparation time: 5 minutes
Cooking time: 3 minutes

*Roasting and grinding spices not only enhances their flavour, but it also prolongs
their shelf life. Using ground roasted spices more than compensates for any
absence of fat.*

225g (8oz) cumin seeds

- Preheat a cast-iron or heavy-based frying pan over medium heat for 2
  minutes. Reduce the heat to very low and add the cumin seeds. Stir them
  continuously for about 1 minute, when the seeds will release their aroma.
  Remove from the heat and tip the seeds out on to a large plate to prevent
  further cooking. Leave to cool.

- Grind the cumin to a powder in a coffee mill. Store in an airtight jar away
  from direct light: this will preserve the warm flavour and aroma of the
  ground cumin for 10–12 weeks.

---

* **HEALTHY HINT:** In India the curative properties of cumin have been
known since ancient times. It is believed to be an effective remedy for
stomach disorders, such as indigestion, diarrhoea and flatulence. Roasted
and ground cumin is added to hot water and blended with honey, then
taken as a cure for colds and the associated aches and pains.

GROUND ROASTED CORIANDER

MAKES 225g
(8oz)

Preparation time: 5 minutes
Cooking time: 3 minutes

Coriander is used in Indian cooking almost every day, either in the form of the dried spice or as the fresh leaves, and it controls the basic flavours of all Indian dishes. Roasting not only enhances the flavours of the spice, it also makes it easier to grind. Roasted ground coriander retains its peak flavour and aroma for many weeks and is sufficiently mellow to complement almost any food. For instant flavour, sprinkle this spice over plain grilled or roasted fish, poultry or meat.

225g (8oz) coriander seeds

- Preheat a cast-iron or heavy-based frying pan over medium heat for 2 minutes. Reduce the heat to very low and add the coriander seeds. Stir them continuously for about 1 minute, when the seeds will release their aroma. Remove from the heat and tip the seeds out on to a large plate to prevent further cooking. Leave to cool.

- Grind the coriander to a powder in a coffee or spice mill. Store in an airtight jar away from direct light: this will preserve the warm flavour and aroma of the ground coriander for 10–12 weeks.

---

* **HEALTHY HINTS: Fresh coriander leaves are used not only to garnish, but also to flavour dishes, for example salads, chutneys and relishes. Although in prepared dishes coriander is eaten in such small quantities that it does not make a significant contribution to the diet, the juice extracted from fresh coriander by pounding or puréeing is rich in vitamins and iron. The seeds are infused in hot water and used as a remedy for digestive disorders and urinary problems.**

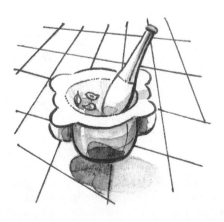

Basic Recipes 21

GARAM MASALA

MAKES 125g
(4½oz)

Preparation time: 15 minutes
Cooking time: 2 minutes

Garam masala is that magic ingredient which instantly transforms an Indian dish with its special zest and warmth. There are many good-quality brands of garam masala which you can use, but I had to share my family recipe with you as I have not found a bought version that can beat this for aroma and flavour. If you are short of time, you can enhance the flavour of bought garam masala by gently roasting it in a heavy pan over low heat for about 1 minute. Just follow your nose – as soon as you smell the aroma released by the spices, remove the pan from the heat and cool the garam masala immediately by spreading it out on a large plate or tray.

15g (½oz) brown cardamom seeds (weight when removed from pods)

15g (½oz) green cardamom seeds (weight when removed from pods)

30g (1oz) cinnamon sticks, broken into small pieces

10g (¼oz) cloves

10g (¼oz) black peppercorns

2 whole nutmegs, about 15g (½oz), lightly crushed

15g (½oz) coriander seeds

15g (½oz) cumin seeds

- Preheat a cast-iron or heavy-based frying pan over medium heat for 1 minute. Reduce the heat to low and add all the spices. Stir for about 1 minute, when the spices will begin to release their aroma. Remove from the heat and transfer to a plate or tray. Set aside to cool.

- Grind the spices to a powder in a coffee or spice mill. Do this in batches and mix them together thoroughly when all the spices are ground. Store in an airtight jar away from direct light. Garam masala will stay fresh for about 12 weeks.

---

* **COOK'S TIP:** Look for plump cardamom pods which are not shrivelled. The seeds inside should be sticky, with a slight gloss. When buying black peppercorns, always look for larger berries as they have much more flavour. Both pepper and nutmeg lose their flavour quickly once ground, so buy them whole and store in airtight jars, away from direct light. To crush a whole nutmeg, place it in a polythene bag and hit it with a rolling pin.

---

* **HEALTHY HINT:** Black pepper is believed to have diuretic and digestive properties. The volatile oil in nutmeg is an important ingredient in creams used to relieve rheumatic pains. Taken in measured quantities, it is also believed to cure insomnia and digestive problems.

AROMATIC STOCK

MAKES 1.5 litres
(2¾ pints)

Yakhni

Preparation time: 10 minutes
Cooking time: 1–1½ hours

Stock is widely used in the Muslim community in India, mainly in rich pilaus and biryanis, also in some meat and poultry recipes. You can achieve a robust flavour without using stock in sauces by adding a few bones when you cook meat and poultry, but for rice dishes you do need a good stock. This stock is easy to make and it keeps well in the refrigerator. If you have to use bought stock, simmer it gently and briefly with the spices listed below, adding a little water to allow for evaporation.

500g (1lb 2oz) chicken and lamb bones

3 x 7.5cm (3in) cinnamon sticks

10 cloves

10 green cardamom pods

1 teaspoon black peppercorns

6 garlic cloves, unpeeled, lightly crushed

7.5cm (3in) cube of fresh root ginger, unpeeled, sliced

1 large onion, unpeeled, quartered

1 parsnip, unpeeled, washed and coarsely chopped

2–3 carrots, unpeeled, washed and coarsely chopped

- Place all the ingredients in a large saucepan and pour in 2.28 litres (4 pints) water. Bring to the boil, then reduce the heat to low, cover the pan and simmer for 1–1½ hours.

- Strain the stock through a muslin-lined sieve. Pour into a heatproof container, cover and set aside to cool.

- Place the stock in the refrigerator as soon as it is cool. It keeps well for more than a month. Boil the stock every 4–5 days, then return it to a clean container. Cover and cool the stock as quickly as possible, then return it to the refrigerator.

- Alternatively, pour the stock into freezer containers, leaving headspace as it expands slightly on freezing, and freeze for up to 6 months.

HEALTHY HINT: As a home remedy, cinnamon infused in hot water brings relief to those suffering from the common cold. The volatile oil in cinnamon is believed to cure gastro-enteritis and associated problems. It is also believed to aid digestion and help prevent nausea. Cardamom is believed to be helpful in reducing acidity and heartburn. This is, perhaps, the reason why cardamom pods coated with edible silver leaf are served after a meal in India. They act as a breath freshener and a digestive rolled

into one. Cloves are highly antiseptic. In India, cloves are used as a remedy for bronchitis, and a clove is chewed to relieve toothache; they are also known to stimulate the digestive system. Together, these three spices are recognized for their ability to create body heat. To fight the bitter winter in the extreme north and the Himalayan region, tea laced with cinnamon, cardamom and cloves is drunk every day.

Snacks & Starters

Within the diversity of Indian cuisine there is an equally varied repertoire of snacks forming an important part of Indian culture. Relaxing over delicious tit-bits with a cup of tea or coffee is the normal way to end a hard day's work and, when friends drop in, a plate of snacks is offered, irrespective of the time of day or night. Children are given tasty morsels in their tiffin or school lunch boxes and there are street vendors who display a variety of tantalizing snacks. When it comes to eating snacks, we simply give in, tempted not only by the sight but also the air that is filled with the aroma of delicious food.

Soups do not feature largely in Indian cooking and the tradition comes mainly from the Mogul era. Spiced soups made from broth are generally served as a drink during a meal. Western influence has changed this tradition to a certain extent and I have created the soups in this section to be serve as a first course.

Starters, as in the western sense, are not a traditional part of an Indian meal. The dishes I find served as starters in British restaurants are those that are eaten as snacks (or side dishes) in India. Indian snacks are versatile. They are ideal with drinks or as side dishes; they can also be served with a relish and bread to make a light lunch or supper. An Indian meal does not consist of several courses. The dishes for the entire meal are served all at once, and diners help themselves to what they want, in the order and quantity they prefer.

VEGETABLE SOUP

SERVES 4

Subzi ka Shorba

Preparation time: 15–20 minutes
Cooking time: 30 minutes

Each serving contains
Kcals: 110
g fat: 3
g saturated fat: 2

This makes an ideal first course on its own or a light meal when served with bread and a relish such as Almond Chutney (see page 183).

450g (1lb) potatoes, coarsely chopped

1–2 green chillies, seeded and chopped

1¼ teaspoons salt or to taste

2 teaspoons Ginger Purée (see page 16)

1 teaspoon Garlic Purée (see page 15)

225g (8oz) closed-cup mushrooms, finely chopped

1 teaspoon paprika

2 spring onions, white part only, finely chopped

1 tablespoon finely chopped fresh coriander leaves

2 tablespoons double cream substitute

- Put the potatoes, chillies and salt in a saucepan and add 450ml (15fl oz) water. Bring to the boil, reduce the heat to medium and cover the pan. Cook for 12–15 minutes or until the potatoes are tender.

- Mash the potatoes lightly in their cooking liquid and add a further 300ml (10fl oz) water. Stir in the ginger and garlic purées, mushrooms and paprika. Bring to the boil, cover and reduce the heat to low. Simmer for 15 minutes.

- Remove from the heat and stir in the spring onions, coriander leaves and cream substitute. Cover the pan and leave the soup to stand for 5 minutes before serving.

FISH TIKKA

Machchi Tikka

**Preparation time: 10-15 minutes, plus marinating
Cooking time: 10 minutes**

Each serving contains
Kcals: 415
g fat: 27
g saturated fat: 8

Delicate salmon may seem an unlikely match for Indian spices, but a carefully chosen, subtle blend of spices enhances the wonderful natural flavour of the fish. The yogurt used in the marinade needs to be the kind with little or no water content. For this you can either strain low-fat plain yogurt through a muslin cloth (this will take 30–40 minutes) or use Greek strained yogurt. You can reduce the fat content further by substituting low-fat yogurt for the crème fraîche.

pinch of saffron threads, pounded

1 tablespoon hot milk

150g (4½oz) low-fat Greek strained yogurt

75g (2½oz) half-fat crème fraîche

1½ tablespoons Ginger Purée (see page 16)

1 tablespoon Garlic Purée (see page 15)

1½ teaspoons salt or to taste

½ teaspoon sugar

1½ tablespoons lemon juice

½ teaspoon ground turmeric

½ teaspoon chilli powder

½ teaspoon Garam Masala (see page 22)

1 teaspoon ground aniseed

675g (1½lb) fresh salmon fillets, skinned and cut into 5cm (2in) cubes

To serve

mild salad onion slices

cucumber slices

crisp lettuce leaves

- Soak the pounded saffron in the hot milk for 10 minutes.

- Put the remaining ingredients, except the fish, in a large bowl. Beat until smooth.

- Stir in the saffron and milk until well mixed, then add the fish. Stir gently until the marinade coats the fish fully. Cover the bowl and set aside in a cool place for 2–3 hours.

- Preheat the grill on high for 10 minutes. Remove the grid from the grill pan and line the pan with aluminium foil. Lightly brush the foil with oil. Brush 4 metal skewers lightly with oil.

- Thread the fish on to the prepared skewers, leaving a slight gap between each piece. Place the skewers on the prepared grill pan and grill them about 7.5cm (3in) away from the heat source for 4–5 minutes.

- Turn the skewers over and spread any remaining marinade over the fish. Cook for a further 4–5 minutes or until the fish is slightly charred. Turn the skewers over two or three times during the last 2 minutes of the cooking time.

- Meanwhile, arrange the mild salad onions, cucumber and lettuce on plates. Place the skewers on the plates and serve immediately.

COURGETTE SOUP

Ghia ka Shorba

Each serving contains
Kcals: 105
g fat: 7
g saturated fat: 5

Preparation time: 10 minutes, plus standing
Cooking time: 10–12 minutes

This super-fast soup tastes delicious hot or chilled. Offer it as a first course or as a light meal when accompanied by hot Tandoori Bread (see page 162).

400g (14oz) courgettes, coarsely chopped

2.5cm (1in) cube of fresh root ginger, peeled and coarsely chopped

1 small green chilli, seeded and chopped

30g (1oz) desiccated coconut

2 tablespoons chopped fresh coriander leaves

1 teaspoon salt or to taste

1 teaspoon sugar

¼ teaspoon freshly ground black pepper

1 tablespoon lime juice

150g (5½oz) low-fat natural yogurt

75ml (2½fl oz) single cream substitute

- Put the courgettes, ginger, chilli and coconut in a saucepan and add 450ml (15fl oz) water. Bring to the boil, cover the pan and reduce the heat to low. Cook for 8–10 minutes.

- Remove the pan from the heat and allow the soup to cool for 5–6 minutes, then purée it until smooth in a blender, adding the remaining ingredients except the cream substitute.

- Return the soup to the rinsed-out saucepan, add the cream substitute and heat gently for 2–3 minutes without boiling.

- Serve immediately, or cool, then chill before serving.

---

* VARIATION: Tender marrow may be used instead of courgettes.

FISH SALAD

Machchi Salat

Preparation time: 10–15 minutes, plus chilling

SERVES 6–8

Each serving contains
Kcals: 150
g fat: 13
g saturated fat: 2.6

My grandmother used to smoke fish to make this salad, which she served with boiled basmati rice and Lentils with Hot Oil Seasoning (see page 142). Whenever I make this salad, I can almost smell the aromas that wafted from my grandmother's kitchen.

250g (9oz) smoked mackerel, skinned

2 tablespoons finely chopped red onions

1 green chilli, seeded and finely chopped

2 tablespoons finely chopped fresh coriander leaves

2 tablespoons lime juice

To serve

an assortment of raw ingredients, such as cucumber slices; short lengths of celery stick; and cherry tomatoes, seeded and pulp removed; or water biscuits

- Coarsely mash the fish with a fork.

- Add the remaining ingredients and chill for 30 minutes.

- Pile small mounds of the mixture on cucumber slices or into celery sticks or cherry tomatoes and serve with a small portion of any bread for a first course. Alternatively, serve on water biscuits with drinks.

---

* **COOK'S TIP: The mixture also makes a delicious sandwich filling. For young children, remove a portion of the salad before adding the chilli.**

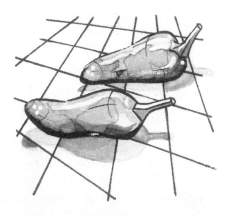

TANDOORI CHICKEN

SERVES 4

Tandoori Murgh

Each serving contains
Kcals: 174
g fat: 5
g saturated fat: 1

**Preparation time: 20–25 minutes, plus marinating
Cooking time: 20 minutes**

One of the most popular Indian dishes, Tandoori Chicken is relatively easy to cook without fat and it is delicious. I prefer tandoori chicken to have the rich golden colour of turmeric with charred patches on the surface, but if you want to add food colouring, you can buy it in powder form from Indian stores. Chaat masala (available from Indian or Pakistani stores) is a spice mix which is sprinkled on hot tandoori chicken – although this is optional, it is worth trying as it transforms the flavour dramatically.

4 chicken joints, skinned

juice of ½ lemon

½ teaspoon salt

75g (2½oz) low-fat Greek strained yogurt

1 small onion, coarsely chopped

1 tablespoon Garlic Purée (see page 15)

1 tablespoon Ginger Purée (see page 16)

½–1 teaspoon chilli powder

2 teaspoons ground coriander

1 teaspoon ground cumin

½ teaspoon Garam Masala (see page 22)

½ teaspoon ground turmeric

1 teaspoon chaat masala (optional)

Garnish

crisp lettuce leaves

cucumber slices

tomatoes slices

onion rings

lemon wedges

- Score the chicken joints all over with a sharp knife, then rub in the lemon juice and salt. Set aside for 15–20 minutes.

- Purée the remaining ingredients, except the chaat masala, in a blender until smooth. Pour the mixture over the chicken and rub in well. Leave to marinate in a covered container for 4–6 hours in a cool place or overnight in the refrigerator. Bring to room temperature before cooking.

- Preheat the grill to high. Line the grill pan (without the rack) with aluminium foil. Place the chicken on the foil, reserving the marinade left in the container. Cook about 12cm (5in) below the heat source for 4–5 minutes. Turn the chicken and cook for a further 4–5 minutes.

• Baste the chicken generously with the reserved marinade and cook nearer the heat source, about 10cm (4in) away, for 5–6 minutes or until charred in patches. Turn the chicken and baste with the remaining marinade. Continue to cook for a further 5–6 minutes or until charred in patches.

• Meanwhile, arrange the garnishing ingredients on a serving dish. Transfer the chicken to the dish and sprinkle with the chaat masala. Serve immediately.

---

* COOK'S TIP: For young children, omit the chilli powder when preparing the marinade, then add it to the marinade before basting and brush it over the portions to be served to adults.

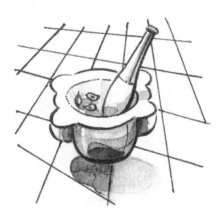

CHICKEN TIKKA

Murgh Tikka

Preparation time: 20 minutes, plus marinating
Cooking time: 12–13 minutes

SERVES 4–5

Each serving contains
Kcals: 360
g fat: 15.5
g saturated fat: 6

Chicken tikka is usually basted with butter or oil during cooking, but a fat-free basting sauce is used in this recipe to keep the chicken moist and succulent.

900g (2lb) chicken breast fillets, skinned and cut into 5cm (2in) cubes

1 tablespoon lemon juice

1¼ teaspoons salt or to taste

pinch of saffron threads, pounded

1 tablespoon hot milk

1 teaspoon sugar

125g (4½oz) low-fat Greek strained yogurt

125ml (4½fl oz) single cream substitute

1 tablespoon Garlic Purée (see page 15)

1 tablespoon Ginger Purée (see page 16)

½ teaspoon ground turmeric

1 teaspoon Garam Masala (see page 22)

½ teaspoon chilli powder

½ teaspoon Ground Roasted Coriander (see page 21)

½ teaspoon Ground Roasted Cumin (see page 20)

2 teaspoons besan (gram or chick-pea flour)

1 tablespoon very finely chopped fresh coriander leaves

- Put the chicken in a bowl and rub the lemon juice and salt well into the pieces. Set aside for 30 minutes.
- Meanwhile, soak the saffron in the milk for 20 minutes.
- Mix the sugar, yogurt, single cream substitute, garlic and ginger purées, turmeric and garam masala. Add to the chicken to coat. Cover and marinate for 3 hours in the refrigerator. Bring to room temperature before cooking.
- Preheat the grill to high and line a grill pan (without the rack) with aluminium foil. Lightly brush the foil and 5–6 metal skewers with oil.
- Thread the chicken on to the skewers, reserving the marinade, and place in the grill pan. Grill 7.5cm (3in) away from the heat for 5 minutes.
- Meanwhile, mix the remaining ingredients with the reserved marinade and brush the chicken with this mixture. Cook for 3–4 minutes.
- Turn the chicken and baste with the remaining marinade. Cook for 2–3 minutes, or until slightly charred. Serve with a green salad.

SILKY CHICKEN KEBABS

Reshmi Kabab

**Preparation time: 10 minutes, plus chilling
Cooking time: 8–10 minutes**

Each serving contains
Kcals: 50
g fat: 2.5
g saturated fat: 0.6

The word resham *means silk and the soft, smooth texture of these kebabs is their main characteristic. They are great with drinks and, if made slightly bigger, they can also be served as a starter, with a relish or salad. Wrapped in chapatis or bought wheat tortillas, and served with a relish, they can make a filling meal.*

55g (2oz) unroasted cashew nut pieces

1 egg

450g (1lb) minced chicken

2 teaspoons Garlic Purée (see page 15)

2 teaspoons Ginger Purée (see page 16)

1–3 green chillies, seeded and chopped

15g (½oz) fresh coriander leaves and stalks

2 teaspoons Ground Roasted Coriander (see page 21)

1 teaspoon Garam Masala (see page 22)

1 teaspoon salt or to taste

Basting sauce

1 tablespoon low-fat plain yogurt

½ teaspoon paprika

¼–½ teaspoon chilli powder

½ teaspoon dried mint

- Blend the cashews and egg in a food processor for a few seconds.

- Add the remaining ingredients (except for the basting sauce) and blend until smooth. Transfer the mixture to a bowl, cover and chill for 30 minutes.

- Preheat the grill to high for 10 minutes. Line a grill pan (without the rack) with aluminium foil and brush it lightly with oil.

- Have a bowl of water ready to wet your fingers before you start shaping the kebabs. This will stop the mixture sticking to your fingers. Wet your fingers and divide the mixture in half, then make 9 portions out of each half.

- Shape each portion into a sausage shape, about 7.5cm (3in) long and place in the prepared grill pan. Dip your fingers in the water occasionally to prevent the mixture from sticking to them.

- Grill the kebabs 7.5cm (3in) below the heat source for 3 minutes. Turn them over and cook for a further 3 minutes.

- Meanwhile, make the basting sauce. Blend the yogurt with 1 tablespoon water until smooth, then mix in all the remaining ingredients and brush generously over the kebabs.

- Cook the kebabs for 1 minute, then turn them over, brush with the remaining basting sauce and cook for a further 1 minute. Serve hot or cold.

---

* COOK'S TIP: If cooking for children as well as adults, omit the chillies and set a portion of the kebab mixture aside, then add the chillies and blend again to make the spicier kebabs.

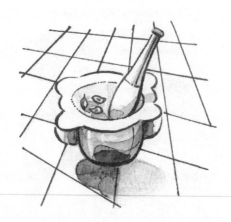

MINCED LAMB KEBABS

SERVES 4

Shami Kabab

Each serving contains
Kcals: 52
g fat: 2.3
g saturated fat: 1

Preparation time: 15–20 minutes, plus chilling
Cooking time: 12–14 minutes

The Indian kabab is said to be a nomadic invention, suited to a roving lifestyle, and brought to India by the Middle Eastern invaders who knew the dish as kebab. Normally, these kebabs are fried, but in this recipe, the ingredients have been adjusted for grilling without added fat and without sacrificing flavour.

75g (2½oz) channa dhal (see page 10)

1–3 dried red chillies

125g (4½oz) low-fat plain yogurt

1 large egg

5cm (2in) cube of fresh root ginger, peeled and coarsely chopped

3–4 garlic cloves, coarsely chopped

2–3 tablespoons chopped fresh coriander leaves

12–15 fresh mint leaves

1–2 green chillies, seeded and chopped

1½ teaspoons Ground Roasted Coriander (see page 21)

1 teaspoon Garam Masala (see page 22)

1 teaspoon salt

1 small onion, coarsely chopped

1 tablespoon lemon juice

500g (1lb 2oz) lean minced lamb

- Wash the channa dhal and soak for 2–3 hours.

- Drain the dhal and put in a saucepan with the red chillies. Add 175ml (6fl oz) water, bring to the boil and reduce the heat to medium-low. Cook, uncovered, for 7–8 minutes or until the liquid has evaporated.

- Put the cooked dhal in a food processor and add the yogurt and egg. Blend until the dhal is fine, then add the remaining ingredients. Blend until smooth. Chill the mixture for 1 hour or overnight in an airtight container.

- Preheat the grill to high for 8–10 minutes and line a grill pan (without the rack) with aluminium foil. Brush the foil lightly with oil.

- Have a bowl of water ready before you start shaping the kebabs. Dip your fingers in the water occasionally as you shape 24 golf-ball-sized portions. Flatten each ball by rotating between your palms, then pressing down gently.

- Place the kebabs in the prepared grill pan and cook them 7.5cm (3in) below the heat source for 3–4 minutes on each side. Serve immediately.

---

* **COOK'S TIP: You can serve these kebabs in pitta bread with a relish of your choice to make a main meal. If you make them bigger than in the above recipe, they can be served with salad as a starter.**

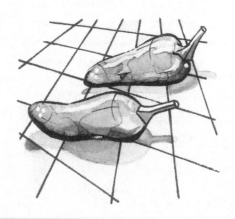

PORK KEBABS

Shikar ka Kabab

Preparation time: 15 minutes
Cooking time: 20 minutes

MAKES 16

Each serving contains
Kcals: 43
g fat: 2
g saturated fat: 0.7

This recipe is based on the idea of wrapping kebabs in leaves and cooking them in a tandoor (clay oven). Banana leaves are traditional, but they have to be thrown away when they have imparted their distinctive flavour to the kebabs. I prefer cabbage leaves because you can eat them, particularly in this recipe, where the kebabs are steamed. The delicious juicy cabbage leaves taste excellent with the superb, subtle flavours of the meat inside.

16 large green cabbage leaves

450g (1lb) lean minced pork

1 tablespoon grated fresh root ginger

1 teaspoon Garlic Purée (see page 15)

1–2 green chillies, seeded and chopped

1 tablespoon finely chopped fresh coriander leaves

2 tablespoons finely chopped red onion

½ teaspoon Garam Masala (see page 22)

1 teaspoon salt or to taste

- Blanch the cabbage leaves in boiling salted water for 5 minutes. Drain and refresh in cold water. Leave to drain in a colander, then pat dry with kitchen paper. Carefully remove the central stem from each leaf without tearing or cutting through the rest of the leaf.

- Combine the meat with the remaining ingredients and knead until smooth. Divide the mixture into 16 equal portions and shape each into a flat cake.

- Place a portion of meat on a cabbage leaf and fold the leaf around it to make a neat parcel. Tie the parcel with string. Repeat with the remaining leaves and portions of meat.

- Prepare a steamer over a saucepan of boiling water. Place the parcels in the steamer and cook for 20 minutes. Serve with Fresh Tomato Chutney (see page 185).

---

* **VARIATION: Use minced chicken or turkey instead of the pork.**

INDIAN CHEESE KEBABS

Paneer ka Kabab

Preparation time: 20 minutes, plus marinating
Cooking time: 10 minutes

SERVES 4–5

Each serving contains
Kcals: 136
g fat: 4
g saturated fat: 1

Here is an attractive and delicious vegetarian tandoori dish which can be cooked under a hot grill. Paneer is full of essential nutrients and has as much protein as meat and poultry – a great source of protein for vegetarians. It is available in large supermarkets and Indian stores. You could use tofu instead, or Cypriot halloumi cheese, but do not use salt with halloumi because, unlike paneer and tofu, it is already salted. You can use either metal or bamboo skewers. If using bamboo, soak them in cold water for 30 minutes to stop them burning under the grill.

200g (7oz) paneer, cut into 2.5cm (1in) cubes (see page 8)

225g (8oz) potatoes, boiled in their skins until tender but still firm, peeled and cut into 2.5cm (1in) cubes

8 shallots, halved

125g (4½oz) red pepper, seeded and cut into 2.5cm (1in) cubes

125g (4½oz) button mushrooms, halved

1 tablespoon sunflower or soya oil

1 teaspoon Ground Roasted Cumin (see page 20)

Marinade

2 tablespoons lemon juice

2 teaspoons Ginger Purée (see page 16)

2 teaspoons Garlic Purée (see page 15)

2 teaspoons ground coriander

½–1 teaspoon chilli powder

½ teaspoon ground turmeric

1 teaspoon salt or to taste

85g (3oz) low-fat plain yogurt

2 teaspoons besan (gram or chick-pea flour), blended to a paste with 2 tablespoons water

Garnish

finely shredded crisp lettuce leaves

cherry tomatoes

- Bring a pan full of water to the boil and add the cubes of paneer. Bring back to the boil and cook for 1 minute. Drain and allow to cool (this enables the cheese to absorb the spices).

- In a large bowl, mix together all the ingredients for the marinade.

- Add the paneer, potatoes, shallots, red pepper and mushrooms and mix thoroughly. Cover with cling film and refrigerate for 3–4 hours. You can leave overnight, but bring it to room temperature before cooking.

- Preheat the grill on high for 5–6 minutes. Remove the grid from the grill pan and line the pan with aluminium foil. Lightly brush the foil with oil.

- Brush 4–5 skewers lightly with oil and thread the marinated paneer and vegetables on to them. Make sure you shake off any excess marinade back into the bowl and alternate the ingredients evenly on the skewers. Place the skewers on the prepared grill pan and grill them about 7.5cm (3in) away from the heat source for 2–3 minutes.

- Add 1 tablespoon water to the marinade left in the bowl and mix it well with the remaining oil. Brush some of the marinade over the kebabs and cook for a further 2–3 minutes. Turn the skewers over and brush with the remaining marinade. Continue to cook for 3–4 minutes or until the kebabs are browned.

- Remove from the heat and sprinkle the cumin evenly over all the skewers. Serve garnished with lettuce leaves and cherry tomatoes.

---

* COOK'S TIP: Besides serving these kebabs as starters, you can make a substantial vegetarian meal by serving them with a lentil dish, and rice or bread.

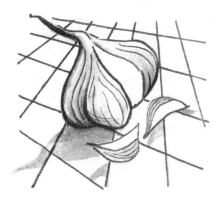

STEAMED PORK BALLS

Shikar Koftas

Preparation time: 25 minutes
Cooking time: 20 minutes

SERVES 6–8

Each serving contains
Kcals: 114
g fat: 5
g saturated fat: 1.8

This is a traditional Tibetan recipe with ravishing flavours. To fit into the low-fat principle of the book, I have omitted the pastry which the Tibetans use to wrap the spiced pork before steaming. Serve the little meatballs with Fresh Tomato Chutney (see page 185) at drinks parties: they will go down a treat.

450g (1lb) lean minced pork

5cm (2in) cube of fresh root ginger, peeled and coarsely chopped

1–2 green chillies, seeded and coarsely chopped

1 teaspoon salt or to taste

1 large egg

4 spring onions, white part only, finely chopped

- Put the pork in a food processor and switch on the machine for a few seconds.

- Add the remaining ingredients, except the spring onions, and process until you have a smooth paste.

- Transfer the mixture to a large bowl and add the spring onions. Mix well.

- Have a bowl of water ready. Dip the fingers of both your hands in the water (this will prevent the meat paste sticking to your fingers) and make small balls, which should be slightly smaller than walnuts. You should be able to make 25–27 meatballs.

- Prepare a steamer over a saucepan of boiling water. Put the meatballs in the steamer and cook for 20 minutes. If you do not have a steamer, put a rack in a saucepan and pour in water to come slightly below the rack. Bring just to the boil. Put the meatballs on a plate and place on the rack. Cover the pan and steam for 20 minutes. Check that the water does not evaporate completely and top up with boiling water if necessary.

- Serve hot or cold (not chilled).

COTTAGE CHEESE CANAPÉS

SERVES 8–10

Paneer Puri

Preparation time: 10–15 minutes

Each serving contains
Kcals: 25
g fat: 0.4
g saturated fat: 0.2

Indian cottage cheese is known as paneer, but I have used low-fat Western cottage cheese for this recipe. Traditionally served on puri, deep-fried crispy bread, I have used water biscuits and sliced cucumber instead.

225g (8oz) low-fat cottage cheese

½ red onion, finely chopped

¼ teaspoon salt or to taste

¼–½ teaspoon chilli powder

¼ teaspoon Ground Roasted Cumin (see page 20)

1 tablespoon finely chopped fresh coriander leaves

To serve

cucumber slices

small water biscuits

Garnish

paprika or chilli powder

Ground Roasted Cumin (see page 20)

- Mix the cottage cheese with the remaining ingredients.

- Carefully spoon the cheese mixture onto cucumber slices and small water biscuits just before serving. Sprinkle with a little paprika or chilli and cumin, and serve immediately.

SPICED POTATO CANAPÉS

SERVES 8–10

Papri Chaat

Preparation time: 20 minutes
Cooking time: 15–20 minutes

Each serving contains
Kcals: 80
g fat: 2
g saturated fat: 0.09

One of the most popular snacks in north India is deep-fried crispy bread topped with potatoes and tamarind sauce. The word chaat *means finger-licking good and even though this is a fat-free version, it is lip-smacking good too!*

225g (8oz) potatoes, boiled in their skins and cooled

125g (4½oz) low-fat plain yogurt

½ teaspoon chilli powder

1 small green chilli, seeded and finely chopped

1 tablespoon finely chopped fresh coriander leaves

1–2 tablespoons finely chopped red onion

½ teaspoon salt or to taste

1 packet small water biscuits

1 quantity Date and Raisin Chutney (see page 184)

- Peel the potatoes and chop them very finely. Put them into a mixing bowl.

- Mix the yogurt with the chilli powder, green chilli, fresh coriander leaves, onion and salt. Pour the mixture over the potatoes and mix thoroughly.

- Pile about 2 teaspoons potato mixture on each biscuit and top with chutney to taste – try a heaped teaspoon first, then adjust the quantity to your liking.

---

* **COOK'S TIP: You can make an instant relish to top the potatoes by mixing 1½ tablespoons tamarind juice with ¼ teaspoon each of chilli powder and salt, and ½ teaspoon each of sugar and Ground Roasted Cumin (see page 20).**

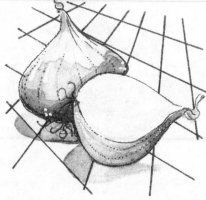

SPICED CORN-ON-THE-COB

Masaledar Bhutta

Preparation time: 10 minutes
Cooking time: 25–30 minutes

Each serving contains
Kcals: 132
g fat: 2.8
g saturated fat: 0.4

Corn is grown extensively in the state of Punjab, where it is used for various delicacies, including corn bread (makki ki roti), the staple on which the people thrive. Here, the cobs of corn are steamed, then brushed with a light seasoning of spice to make a delicious snack or starter. They can also be cooked on the barbecue; whichever cooking method is used, always wrap the corn in aluminium foil to prevent the cobs from drying out.

4 large cobs of corn

juice of 1 lime

½ teaspoon salt

½ teaspoon Ground Roasted Cumin (see page 20)

½ teaspoon chilli powder or to taste

¼ teaspoon dried mint

- Prepare a steamer over a saucepan of boiling water. Wrap the corn individually in aluminium foil and place in the steamer. Cook for 25–30 minutes.

- Meanwhile, mix the lime juice with the remaining ingredients. Brush the spice mixture over the corn and serve immediately.

STUFFED PEPPERS

Bharwan Simla Mirchi

Preparation time: 15–20 minutes
Cooking time: 20–25 minutes

SERVES 4

Each serving contains
Kcals: 196
g fat: 7
g saturated fat: 0.8

With its striking appearance, this simple and nutritious vegetarian starter cannot fail to tempt. The peppers can also make a main meal for two if served with a salad and Puffed Grilled Bread (see page 161) or Spiced Chapatis (see page 160).

2 green or red peppers

1½ tablespoons sunflower or soya oil

½ teaspoon black mustard seeds

½ teaspoon cumin seeds

1 small red onion, finely chopped

1 green or red chilli, seeded and chopped

¼ teaspoon ground turmeric

½ teaspoon chilli powder (optional)

1 teaspoon Ground Roasted Coriander (see page 21)

400g (14oz) can chick peas, drained and rinsed

¼–½ teaspoon salt

2 tablespoons finely chopped fresh coriander leaves

1 tablespoon lime juice

1 tablespoon wholemeal flour

To serve

cucumber slices

lettuce leaves

- Carefully halve the peppers lengthways keeping the pieces of stalk intact in both halves. Remove the seeds and the pith and brush the skin lightly with oil. Set aside.

- Preheat the oven to 190C°/375°F/Gas 5. Line a roasting tin with foil.

- Heat the remaining oil in a non-stick saucepan over low heat and add the mustard seeds. When they crackle, add the cumin seeds then the onion and chilli. Increase the heat and fry for 3–4 minutes, stirring.

- Reduce the heat to low and add the turmeric, chilli powder (if using) and ground coriander. Cook for 30 seconds, then add the chick peas. Cook for 1 minute and add the salt, coriander leaves and lime juice. Stir to mix well.

- Pour in 75ml (2½fl oz) water and add the flour. Stir until the water has been absorbed. Remove from the heat and divide the mixture among the pepper halves. Place on the prepared roasting tin.

- Cook for 15 minutes and serve with cucumber and lettuce.

Fish Dishes

India has a vast coastline and the entire land is latticed with rivers and lakes, so it is not surprising that the country has a thriving industry specializing in exporting some of the finest-quality seafood. Indian cooks take full advantage of the abundant supply of fish to create an extensive repertoire of recipes, but I am always saddened by the lack of fish and seafood dishes on menus in Indian restaurants in Britain.

Buying and storing fish properly are just as important as cooking it successfully. Always make sure that the fish is absolutely fresh: the most obvious sign of freshness is the eyes, which should be shiny and full. Fish should look moist and glistening, and feel firm to the touch. Never leave fish at room temperature, even for a short time, but store it promptly in the refrigerator. Cook fish as soon as possible after purchase, ideally on the same day.

Fish is a highly nutritious protein food, and white fish is low in fat. Oily fish, such as salmon and mackerel, contain fats which contribute to healthy eating. Recent research indicates that the omega-3 fatty acids found in oily fish offer protection against coronary diseases.

ARUNACHAL FISH CURRY

Pa Chao

Preparation time: 15–20 minutes, plus standing
Cooking time: 10 minutes

Each serving contains
Kcals: 315
g fat: 20
g saturated fat: 6

When I was in India recently, my friend Fantry Jaswal cooked this fish curry for me. Fantry comes from the beautiful district of Arunachal Pradesh in the Himalayan foothills and it is from her that I learned to appreciate the flavours of tribal food. I modified the recipe slightly, but it retains the original characteristics. Use any firm white fish instead of salmon.

4 salmon steaks, halved

1 teaspoon salt or to taste

1 tablespoon lemon juice

¼–½ teaspoon chilli powder

½ teaspoon ground turmeric

175g (6oz) canned chopped tomatoes with their juice
or fresh tomatoes, skinned and chopped

15g (½oz) fresh coriander leaves and stalks

1–2 green chillies, seeded and chopped

1 large garlic clove, coarsely chopped

2.5cm (1in) cube of fresh root ginger, peeled and coarsely chopped

30g (1oz) desiccated coconut

• Lay the pieces of fish on a large plate and sprinkle with half the salt, the lemon juice, chilli powder and turmeric. Rub gently with your fingertips and set aside for 15–20 minutes.

• Purée the remaining ingredients, except the coconut, in a blender. Grind the coconut in a spice or coffee mill until smooth.

• Put the puréed ingredients in a non-stick saucepan, about 30cm (12in) in diameter, and add the coconut and remaining salt. Heat over low heat, stirring, until heated through.

• Add the fish to the pan in a single layer on the sauce. Cover and cook for 7–8 minutes. Shake the pan from side to side two or three times and spoon some of the hot sauce over the fish.

• Remove from the heat and serve with boiled basmati rice and Cabbage with Ginger (see page 169).

---

* **COOK'S TIP: It is important to grind the coconut so that you have a smooth sauce. If you do not have a coffee mill, soak the coconut in boiling water (just enough to cover it), then drain it and add to the ingredients in the blender. It will take longer to achieve a smooth texture in the blender.**

FISH WITH LENTIL SAUCE

SERVES 4

Dhan-Dhal-Patio

Preparation time: 15–20 minutes
Cooking time: 30–35 minutes

Each serving contains
Kcals: 240
g fat: 6.6
g saturated fat: 0.85

This is one of the superb contributions made to Indian cuisine by a small community known as the Parsees who came to India about thirteen centuries ago from their Persian homeland. A little oil is necessary here to achieve the authentic flavour. Served with boiled basmati rice, this makes a complete meal, especially when accompanied by a salad or raita for a healthy balance.

2 tablespoons sunflower or soya oil

½ teaspoon cumin seeds

2 teaspoons Garlic Purée (see page 15)

2 teaspoons Ginger Purée (see page 16)

125g (4½oz) red lentils, washed and drained

½ teaspoon ground turmeric

1 green chilli, seeded and chopped

375ml (13½fl oz) warm water

1 teaspoon salt or to taste

½ onion, finely chopped

125g (4½oz) tomatoes, skinned and chopped

½ teaspoon Ground Roasted Cumin (see page 20)

½ teaspoon Ground Roasted Coriander (see page 21)

½ teaspoon chilli powder

¼ teaspoon Garam Masala (see page 22)

½ teaspoon tamarind concentrate or 1 tablespoon tamarind juice

½ teaspoon sugar

400g (14oz) peeled raw king prawns

2 tablespoons finely chopped fresh coriander leaves

boiled basmati rice to serve

- Heat half the oil in a non-stick pan over low heat. Add the cumin seeds, followed by half the garlic and ginger purées. Fry for 1 minute.

- Add the lentils, half the turmeric and the chilli. Increase the heat slightly and fry for 2–3 minutes, stirring constantly.

- Pour in 325ml (11½fl oz) of the water and bring to the boil. Reduce the heat to low, cover the pan and cook for 25–30 minutes. Add a little more water (in addition to the total quantity in the ingredients list) if necessary; the dhal should resemble a thick batter when cooked. Stir in half the salt and remove from the heat.

- While the lentils are cooking, heat the remaining oil in a non-stick saucepan over medium heat. Add the onion and the remaining garlic and ginger purées. Fry for 2 minutes, then reduce the heat slightly and continue to fry for a further 1–2 minutes.

- Stir in the tomatoes, cumin, ground coriander, chilli powder, garam masala and the remaining turmeric. Cook for 2 minutes, then add the remaining 50ml (1¾fl oz) water. Continue to cook for 2–3 minutes, stirring frequently.

- Stir in the remaining salt, the tamarind and sugar. If using tamarind concentrate, stir until it has dissolved.

- Add the prawns, increase the heat slightly and cook for 5–7 minutes, stirring frequently. Sprinkle in a little water if necessary. Add the fresh coriander leaves and remove from the heat.

- Serve a portion of dhal on boiled basmati rice and top with the prawns.

---

* **COOK'S TIP: You can use any firm white fish or prawns. I have used raw king prawns, but cooked small or king prawns can be used – simply toss them gently in the spices until heated through. If you cannot get either tamarind concentrate or juice, use 1 tablespoon lime juice.**

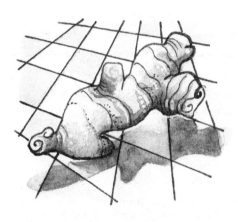

BAKED FISH

Dum Machchi

Preparation time: 10 minutes
Cooking time: 1 hour

Each serving contains
Kcals: 215
g fat: 5
g saturated fat: 1.5

This makes an easy and tasty mid-week meal. It takes only a few minutes to combine the ingredients, then the dish is simply placed in the oven and you are free to relax with your favourite pre-dinner tipple.

550g (1¼lb) cod or haddock fillet, skinned and cut in chunks

225g (8oz) potatoes, boiled and coarsely chopped

2.5cm (1in) cube of fresh root ginger, coarsely chopped

2 large garlic cloves, coarsely chopped

1–2 green chillies, seeded and chopped

15g (½oz) fresh coriander leaves and stalks

1 teaspoon salt or to taste

½ teaspoon ground aniseed

½ teaspoon ground turmeric

2 large eggs

150ml (5fl oz) semi-skimmed milk

2 teaspoons chopped fresh dill

¼ red pepper, seeded and finely chopped

- Preheat the oven to 190°C/375°F/ Gas 5.

- Blend all the ingredients, except the dill and red pepper, in a food processor until smooth.

- Lightly brush a 23cm (9in) non-stick ring mould with oil and sprinkle the base of the ring with the dill and red pepper.

- Pack the fish mixture into the ring and bake for 1 hour or until the top is lightly browned.

- Use a knife to loosen the edge of the fish mixture around the rim of the mould. Cover the top of the mould with a serving platter, then invert both platter and mould. Lift off the mould. Serve immediately, with Kohlrabi Salad (see page 189) and any bread.

---

* **COOK'S TIP: The mixture can be puréed in a blender, but you will have to do it in batches, then mix them all together in a bowl.**

DRY-SPICED GRILLED FISH

SERVES 4

Sukha Masaledar Machchi

Preparation time: 10 minutes, plus marinating
Cooking time: 7–8 minutes

Each serving contains
Kcals: 296
g fat: 19
g saturated fat: 3

If you are a fish lover, you will find this delicately spiced dish to be divine. Succulent chunks of salmon perfumed with coriander and a touch of chilli and garlic will leave you craving for more! You do need oily fish for this – my second choice is rainbow trout when salmon steaks are not available.

2 tablespoons lemon juice

1 teaspoon Garlic Purée (see page 15)

1 teaspoon Ginger Purée (see page 16)

¼–½ teaspoon chilli powder

½ teaspoon salt

4 salmon steaks

1 tablespoon sunflower or soya oil

1½ teaspoons Ground Roasted Coriander (see page 21)

1 tablespoon very finely chopped fresh coriander leaves

- Mix the lemon juice, garlic and ginger purées, chilli and salt.

- Lay the salmon steaks on a large plate or dish and gently rub the seasoning mixture into them. Cover and set aside to marinate for 30 minutes.

- Preheat the grill to high and line a grill pan (without the rack) with aluminium foil. Brush the foil lightly with oil and arrange the prepared fish on the foil.

- Cook the fish about 12cm (5in) away from the heat source for 3–4 minutes.

- Meanwhile, mix the oil, ground coriander and fresh coriander together. Turn the fish over, taking care not to break the steaks. Divide the coriander mixture equally among the steaks, spreading it gently to cover them completely.

- Grill the salmon for a further 2–3 minutes, then serve immediately. The salmon steaks are delicious served with Savoury Potato Mash (see page 165) and Almond Chutney (see page 183) or a lentil dish and Cinnamon Rice (see page 147).

FISH CAKES

Machchi Tikki

**Preparation time: 20–25 minutes, plus chilling
Cooking time: 12–15 minutes**

Each serving contains
Kcals: 80
g fat: 2.3
g saturated fat: 0.4

You will need a heavy non-stick frying pan to cook these delicious fish cakes, as only a little oil is brushed lightly over it and the fish cakes are cooked until browned. Make half the quantity if you wish to serve them as a starter; shaped into cocktail-size cakes, they are also a delicious savoury to serve with drinks.

2 thick slices of white bread, 1–2 days old, crusts removed and cut into cubes

1 large egg

2.5cm (1in) cube of fresh root ginger, peeled and chopped

2 large garlic cloves, chopped

3 tablespoons coarsely chopped fresh coriander leaves and stalks

1–2 green chillies, seeded and chopped

550g (1¼lb) white fish fillet, skinned

125g (4½oz) potatoes, boiled and coarsely chopped

½ teaspoon ground aniseed

¼ teaspoon ground turmeric

1 teaspoon salt or to taste

1 small onion, coarsely chopped

1½ tablespoons sunflower or soya oil

- Put the bread in a food processor and add the egg, ginger, garlic, fresh coriander and chillies. Process until smooth.

- Add the remaining ingredients, except the oil, and blend by pulsing the power on and off until the mixture has a slightly coarse texture. Transfer the mixture to a suitable container, cover and chill for 30 minutes.

- Divide the mixture in half and shape 6 equal-sized cakes, about 5mm (¼in) thick, from each half.

- Heat a heavy non-stick frying pan over medium heat and brush a little oil over the entire surface. Heat again for 1–2 minutes, then cook the fish cakes in batches, adding a little extra oil as necessary and spreading it with a brush each time. Allow 2–3 minutes on each side or until the fish cakes are browned.

- Serve with Spinach Raita (see page 182) or Fresh Tomato Chutney (see page 185) and any bread.

FISH IN COCONUT MILK

SERVES 4

Meen Molee

Preparation time: 10–15 minutes
Cooking time: 10–12 minutes

Each serving contains
Kcals: 340
g fat: 23
g saturated fat: 9

This is adapted from a south-Indian recipe for which onions, ginger, chillies and spices are sautéed in coconut oil before adding coconut milk and fish. To balance this oil-free version, I have also omitted many of the traditional spices and I am delighted with the subtle, but brilliant, flavours. Use firm-fleshed white fish, such as swordfish, shark, monkfish or cod, or king prawns instead of salmon.

45g (1½oz) coconut milk powder

240ml (8fl oz) boiling water

20 curry leaves, preferably fresh

5mm (¼in) cube of fresh root ginger, peeled and cut into julienne strips

1 teaspoon chilli powder or to taste

½ teaspoon salt or to taste

4 salmon steaks, halved

2–3 fresh chillies, preferably red

1 tablespoon chopped fresh coriander leaves

1 tablespoon lime juice

• Blend the coconut milk powder with the hot water and put into a saucepan, about 30cm (12in) in diameter, with the curry leaves, ginger, chilli powder and salt. Heat until simmering, and simmer for 2–3 minutes.

• Add the fish, laying the pieces in the pan in a single layer, and bring slowly back to simmering point. Cover the pan and cook over low heat for 5–6 minutes. Shake the pan from side to side occasionally, but do not stir the curry.

• Add the whole chillies, fresh coriander and lime juice. Shake the pan as before and simmer for 1–2 minutes. Remove from the heat and serve immediately, with boiled basmati rice and Cabbage Salad (see page 187).

---

* **COOK'S TIP: When halving salmon steaks, use a heavy knife (and tap it down with a rolling pin) or poultry shears to cut through the bone. Leaving the bone in helps to keep the fish in shape during cooking.**

FISH IN MUSTARD SAUCE

Shorshe diya Maach

SERVES 4

Each serving contains
Kcals: 145
g fat: 1.3
g saturated fat: 0.18

Preparation time: 10–15 minutes, plus marinating
Cooking time: 10–12 minutes

A speciality from Bengal and Assam, this dish is traditionally cooked in pungent mustard oil with ground mustard. My grandmother always steamed the marinated fish wrapped in banana leaf which imparted a distinctive flavour. Here, I have omitted the oil and used mustard powder, then wrapped the fish in aluminium foil – the result captures most of the traditional flavours and appearance. Large whole sardines are also excellent prepared in this way.

675g (1½lb) cod, haddock or halibut fillet, skinned

1½ tablespoons mustard powder

1½ teaspoons besan (gram or chick-pea flour)

½ teaspoon ground turmeric

1 teaspoon salt or to taste

2–3 tablespoons finely chopped fresh coriander leaves and stalks

1 red chilli, seeded and cut into julienne strips

1 green chilli, seeded and cut into julienne strips

- Cut the fish into 5cm (2in) pieces and place on a large plate.

- Mix the mustard powder and besan together, then blend to a smooth paste with 2 tablespoons water. If there are any tiny lumps (besan can become lumpy) strain the paste through a fine sieve or strainer.

- Add the turmeric, salt and fresh coriander to the besan paste and mix thoroughly. Spread the paste evenly on the fish, cover and marinate in the refrigerator for 1–2 hours.

- When you are ready to cook the fish, prepare a steamer over a saucepan of boiling water.

- Put half of the fish fillets on a large piece of aluminium foil and arrange half of the chillies on top. Cover with the remaining fish and place the remaining chillies on top. Fold the foil around the fish to enclose it in a neat parcel, folding and pinching the edges to seal them well.

- Place in the steamer and cook for 10–12 minutes. Serve immediately, with boiled basmati rice and Mixed Vegetable Curry (see page 173).

FISH IN COCONUT AND CORIANDER SAUCE

Mashli Ghashi

Preparation time: 10–15 minutes, plus marinating
Cooking time: 12–15 minutes

Each serving contains
Kcals: 370
g fat: 26
g saturated fat: 9

This classic dish from the southern coastal region of India is usually prepared with a generous amount of freshly grated coconut, but I have given it an entirely modern taste and reduced the coconut to an acceptable level for a healthy diet. Dill complements salmon so perfectly that I have added it to the sauce, and the transformation in taste and appearance is superb.

4 salmon steaks, halved

1 tablespoon lemon juice

¼ teaspoon ground turmeric

1 teaspoon salt or to taste

1 tablespoon sunflower or soya oil

1 teaspoon Ginger Purée (see page 16)

1 teaspoon Garlic Purée (see page 15)

45g (1½oz) coconut milk powder

225ml (7½fl oz) very hot water

½–1 teaspoon chilli powder

1 teaspoon Ground Roasted Coriander (see page 21)

1 teaspoon dried dill

- Lay the fish on a flat dish and sprinkle with the lemon juice, turmeric and half the salt. Gently rub the seasonings into the fish with your finger tips, then set it aside to marinate for 10 minutes.

- Heat the oil in a non-stick saucepan or frying pan, at least 30cm (12in) in diameter, over low heat. Add the ginger and garlic purées and fry for 1 minute.

- Blend the coconut milk powder with the hot water and add to the pan, followed by the remaining salt, chilli powder and coriander.

- Lay the salmon steaks in the pan in a single layer. Wait until the sauce begins to bubble gently, then cover the pan and increase the heat slightly. Cook for 3–4 minutes.

- Remove the lid and cook for a further 3–4 minutes, then shake the pan from side to side and continue to cook for a further 2–3 minutes.

- Sprinkle with the dill, then stir gently to mix and remove from the heat. Serve immediately, with boiled basmati rice and Spiced Green Beans (see page 174).

LEAF-WRAPPED FISH

SERVES 4

Patra-ni-Machchi

Preparation time: 30 minutes
Cooking time: 15 minutes

*This traditional dish was contributed to Indian cuisine by the Parsee community.
Traditionally, the fish, with a chutney made of fresh coriander leaves and coconut, is
wrapped in a banana leaf, then steamed. The banana leaf imparts a distinctive
flavour. I have used cabbage leaves and omitted the coconut in this version.*

8 large leaves of Savoy cabbage

4 salmon steaks, halved

2–3 tomatoes, sliced, to garnish

Chutney

30g (1oz) blanched almonds

30g (1oz) sunflower seeds

125ml (4½fl oz) boiling water

30g (1oz) fresh coriander leaves and stalks, coarsely chopped

1–2 green chillies, seeded and coarsely chopped

2 large garlic cloves, coarsely chopped

2.5cm (1in) cube of fresh root ginger, coarsely chopped

1½ tablespoons lemon juice

½ teaspoon salt or to taste

1 teaspoon sugar

- For the chutney, soak the almonds and sunflower seeds in the hot water for 10–15 minutes.

- Meanwhile, blanch the cabbage leaves in boiling salted water for 5 minutes. Drain and refresh in cold water, then drain again and pat dry with kitchen paper. Carefully cut out and discard the hard stalks from the base of each leaf.

- Put all the remaining ingredients for the chutney in a blender or food processor. Add the almonds and sunflower seeds, along with the water in which they were soaked, and process until smooth. Divide the chutney into 8 equal portions.

- Spread half a portion of chutney on a piece of fish and place it, chutney-side down, on a cabbage leaf. Spread the remainder of the portion of chutney on top. Carefully wrap the leaf around the fish to make a neat parcel and tie it up with string, criss-crossing it around the parcel and making sure there are no gaps. Repeat with the remaining fish, cabbage and chutney.

- Prepare a steamer over a saucepan of boiling water. Place the prepared

From the top: Fresh Tomato Chutney (page 185), Fish Tikka (page 28), Steamed Pork Balls (page 42) and Indian Cheese Kebabs (page 40).

Fruit Curry (page 176) and Saffron Rice (page 148).

Baked Kebabs (page 104) and Fruit Raita (page 179).

Lentils with Kidney Beans (page 132) and Tandoori Bread (page 162).

Chicken in Apricot Juice (page 70), Carrots and Green Beans with Poppy Seeds (page 170) and Spiced Chapatis (page160).

Spiced Pork Chops (page 120) with Aubergine Pilau (page 156) and Pineapple Raita (page 178).

King Prawns with Baby Courgettes (page 63) and Cumin-Coriander Rice (page 146).

Spiced Pears (page 198).

parcels in the steamer and steam for 15 minutes.

● To serve, carefully remove the string from the parcels and garnish with the sliced tomatoes. Serve immediately. Savoury Potato Mash (see page 165) or Spiced Sweet Potatoes (see page 167) are delicious with the parcels. Alternatively, serve with Fried Brown Rice (see page 149) and Lentils with Hot Oil Seasoning (see page 142).

FISH IN TAMARIND JUICE

Imli ki Machchi

Preparation time: 10–15 minutes
Cooking time: 20 minutes

Each serving contains
Kcals: 585
g fat: 46
g saturated fat: 14

This recipe is adapted from one of my late mother-in-law's wonderful creations, a dish typical of the southern coastal district of Karnataka.

40g (1½oz) coconut milk powder

350ml (11fl oz) hot water

½ teaspoon ground turmeric

1–1¼ teaspoons chilli powder

½ teaspoon concentrated tamarind pulp or 1 tablespoon tamarind juice (see page 9)

½–1 teaspoon salt

900g (2lb) mackerel fillets

Hot Oil Seasoning

1 tablespoon sunflower or soya oil

2 teaspoons Garlic Purée (see page 15)

1 tablespoon ground coriander

6–8 fresh or dried curry leaves

- Blend the coconut milk powder with the hot water and pour the mixture into a large saucepan, about 30cm (12in) in diameter.

- Add the turmeric, chilli powder, tamarind and salt. Bring to a slow simmer and cook, uncovered, for 5 minutes. Stir to dissolve the tamarind.

- Meanwhile, cut each mackerel fillet across into 3 pieces. Add to the sauce.

- When the sauce bubbles, reduce the heat to low and simmer for 6–8 minutes.

- During the last 3–4 minutes of cooking time for the fish, prepare the hot oil seasoning. Heat the oil in a small saucepan over low heat. Add the garlic purée and cook gently for 1 minute, then add the coriander and curry leaves. Cook for 30 seconds before adding the mixture to the fish curry.

- Shake the pan gently from side to side to ensure that the seasoning is evenly distributed. Serve immediately with boiled basmati rice and Spiced Green Beans (see page 174) or Dry-Spiced Okra (see page 168).

---

* **COOK'S TIP:** Concentrated tamarind looks and behaves like black treacle – when measuring it out, it will slide off a lightly greased spoon easily.

---

* **HEALTHY HINT:** Mackerel is rich in omega-3 fatty acids which are beneficial to the heart.

60 *Fat Free Indian Cookery*

TANDOORI-STYLE FISH

SERVES 2

Tandoori Machchi

Preparation time: 15–20 minutes, plus marinating
Cooking time: 12–15 minutes

Each serving contains
Kcals: 226
g fat: 8.7
g saturated fat: 1.3

Fish and seafood cooked in a tandoor (clay oven) take on a characteristic flavour and appearance. Tandoori recipes are great for barbecuing or they can be cooked in a very hot oven or under the grill until the food is slightly charred, when they look very similar to the authentic dish. However, it is hard to replicate the flavours achieved by the tandoori combination of clay and charcoal cooking. In India, the most popular fish for tandoori cooking is pomfret, a firm-fleshed fish found in the Arabian sea. Lemon sole, plaice and trout also work very well.

2 rainbow trout, cleaned with heads and tails on

1 tablespoon lemon juice

½ teaspoon salt

55g (2oz) Greek strained yogurt

2 teaspoons Ginger Purée (see page 16)

2 teaspoons Garlic Purée (see page 15)

½ teaspoon sugar

½ teaspoon ground aniseed

½ teaspoon ground turmeric

½ teaspoon Garam Masala (see page 22)

½ teaspoon chilli powder

2 teaspoons besan (gram or chick-pea flour)

1 tablespoon finely chopped fresh coriander leaves

½ green chilli, seeded and finely chopped

Garnish

sliced spring onions

shredded lettuce leaves

lemon wedges

- Make three or four diagonal slits on both sides of each fish. Gently rub the lemon juice and salt into the fish. Place in a large shallow dish and set aside for 15–20 minutes.

- Place the remaining ingredients, except the fresh coriander leaves and green chilli, in a mixing bowl and beat with a wire whisk until smooth.

- Pour the mixture over the fish and rub it gently into them, making sure you rub the mixture into the slits and the stomach cavity. Cover and marinate in the refrigerator for 2–3 hours.

Fish Dishes 61

- Preheat the grill on high for 10 minutes. Line a grill pan (without the rack) with aluminium foil and brush it lightly with oil.

- Place the fish on the foil and cook 7.5cm (3in) away from the heat source for 6–7 minutes or until slightly charred. Turn the fish over and continue to cook for a further 5–6 minutes or until charred on the second side.

- Add the fresh coriander leaves and chilli to the cooking juices in the grill pan and spoon them over the fish. Transfer to serving plates and add the garnishing ingredients.

- Serve immediately, with a raita and any bread to complete the meal.

---

* COOK'S TIP: Low-fat plain yogurt can be used instead of Greek strained yogurt, but you will need to strain it through a muslin-lined sieve over a bowl to remove excess moisture. This will take 25–30 minutes and you will need double the quantity of yogurt because it reduces considerably by the time it is strained.

KING PRAWNS WITH BABY COURGETTES

SERVES 2–4

Jhinga aur Ghia

Preparation time: 10 minutes
Cooking time: 10 minutes

Each serving contains
Kcals: 240
g fat: 15
g saturated fat: 12

Succulent king prawns and baby courgettes look really striking together. The characteristic taste here comes from freshly grated root ginger and curry leaves, which have the most captivating flavour combined with an enticing aroma. This quantity will serve two people as a main meal with Cumin-Coriander Rice (see page 146) or boiled basmati rice. Served with rice plus a lentil and a vegetable dish, it will easily feed four.

If you are generally following a low-fat diet, you can certainly indulge yourself occasionally. As this recipe has a higher fat content, perhaps you could treat yourself on a Sunday or cook it for a special dinner party.

225g (8oz) baby courgettes

40g (1½oz) coconut milk powder

175ml (6fl oz) boiling water

½ teaspoon ground aniseed

1 teaspoon grated fresh root ginger

½ teaspoon salt or to taste

½ teaspoon crushed dried red chillies

12–16 fresh or dried curry leaves

225g (8oz) peeled cooked king prawns

1 tablespoon lime juice

1 tablespoon finely chopped fresh coriander leaves

- Slit the courgettes lengthways in half and set aside.

- Blend the coconut milk powder with the boiling water and add the ground aniseed, ginger, salt and crushed chillies. Mix well.

- Put the courgettes in a wide shallow pan and add the blended coconut milk and the curry leaves. Place over medium-low heat, bring to a slow simmer and cook, uncovered, for 5 minutes.

- Add the prawns, cover and cook for 5 minutes. Stir in the lime juice and fresh coriander and remove from the heat. Serve at once.

Chicken
Dishes

Chicken is lower in fat than other types of meat and the modest amount of fat it does contain is unsaturated, so it is the ideal meat for a low-fat diet. Chicken is also a good source of minerals, some B vitamins and protein. Thigh meat has plenty of zinc, which is necessary for the efficient functioning of the immune system and essential for growth and reproduction.

The highest fat content in chicken is in the skin and in Indian cooking the skin is always removed. Removing the skin also allows the flavours of spices and other ingredients to penetrate deeper. The use of yogurt, milk and fruit juices in cooking tenderizes the meat by breaking up the muscle fibres. This further enhances the flavour and texture of the finished dish.

You can buy skinned chicken, but this can be expensive, and it is not really difficult to skin chicken. The majority of recipes call for chicken thighs or breasts and these are easier to skin than a whole chicken. Use a cloth to hold the skin as you pull it back off the flesh as this prevents slipping, making the task easier and quicker. I have a 'meat cloth' which I use specifically for this task – I wash it with normal detergent immediately after use and also rinse it in a gentle bleach solution before thoroughly rinsing in clean water. When it is completely dry, I store it in a plastic bag, sealed with a wire tie, so it is ready for use next time.

Turkey is also low in fat and I have included one turkey recipe in this section; you can use turkey breast in other recipes, instead of chicken, if you like.

Cooking temperatures are very important and gentle heat is the key to successful meat and poultry cooking. Once the chicken is tender, you can reduce the sauce, if necessary, by turning the heat up. Remove the meat from the sauce and keep it hot while you reduce the sauce to the required consistency.

Unless otherwise stated, the dishes in this section can be frozen. Make sure you cool the dish quickly by transferring it to a cooling tray (a large roasting tin is ideal). Once cooled, transfer it to a suitable freezer container, then label and chill it before placing in the freezer. Always thaw frozen dishes slowly in the refrigerator, and reheat them gently, but thoroughly, to ensure that the food is piping hot. You may have to add a little warm water occasionally during reheating to prevent a sauce from becoming too dry.

For dry dishes, which do not have a sauce, thaw them as above, then wrap in double-thick foil and place in a preheated oven at 180°C/350°F/Gas 4 until completely reheated – allow 15–30 minutes, depending on the type and size of dish.

CHICKEN IN YOGURT

Dahi Murgh

Preparation time: 15 minutes
Cooking time: 45–50 minutes

Each serving contains
Kcals: 240
g fat: 9
g saturated fat: 3

This dish is adapted from a traditional recipe. Cooking chicken gently in yogurt without any additional liquid results in a delicious, concentrated flavour.

1 large onion, finely sliced

1 teaspoon salt or to taste

2 teaspoons Ginger Purée (see page 16)

2 teaspoons Garlic Purée (see page 15)

½ teaspoon ground turmeric

½–1 teaspoon chilli powder

2 teaspoons Ground Roasted Coriander (see page 21)

1½ teaspoons Ground Roasted Cumin (see page 20)

125g (4½oz) low-fat plain yogurt

8 chicken thighs, skinned

1 teaspoon sugar

2 x 2.5cm (1in) pieces of cinnamon stick

4 green cardamom pods, bruised

4 whole cloves

1 tablespoon tomato purée

½ teaspoon Garam Masala (see page 22)

2 tablespoons chopped fresh coriander leaves

- Cook the onion and salt in a non-stick saucepan over low heat for 2–3 minutes. Increase the heat to medium and continue cooking, stirring frequently, for a further 2–3 minutes or until the onion is soft. The salt draws out the natural juices from the onions, so that they can be cooked without added fat and without burning. Reduce the heat slightly towards the end of cooking, if necessary.

- Stir in the ginger and garlic purées, turmeric, chilli powder, coriander and cumin. Cook for 1 minute, then add half the yogurt to moisten the spices. Stir and cook for a further minute.

- Add the chicken, sugar, cinnamon, cardamoms, cloves and the remaining yogurt. Stir to mix thoroughly, then cover the pan, reduce the heat to low and cook for 35–40 minutes, stirring occasionally.

- Stir in the tomato purée, garam masala and coriander leaves, and simmer for 2–3 minutes. Serve with boiled basmati rice or Fried Brown Rice (see page 149) and Cabbage Salad (see page 187).

CHICKEN IN MILK

Murgh Shafak Sheer

Preparation time: 15 minutes, plus cooling the spices
Cooking time: 40–45 minutes

SERVES 4

Each serving contains
Kcals: 261
g fat: 10
g saturated fat: 3

I have adapted this recipe for healthy eating from a rather exotic dish created in the style of the Indian Royal House of Sailana. In his book, Cooking Delights of the Maharajas, *Maharaja Digvijaya Singh gives an insight into this fascinating style of cooking. I have omitted ghee and used chicken instead of mutton for my version, which is less rich than the Maharaja's opulent creation, but retains much of its fabulous flavour.*

2 teaspoons coriander seeds

1½ teaspoons cumin seeds

½ teaspoon black peppercorns

2–4 dried red chillies, chopped

1 tablespoon sunflower seeds

675g (1½lb) boneless chicken breasts or thighs, skinned

2 teaspoons Ginger Purée (see page 16)

2 teaspoons Garlic Purée (see page 15)

1 large onion, finely sliced

2 x 2.5cm (1in) pieces of cinnamon stick

6 green cardamom pods, bruised

1 teaspoon salt or to taste

½ teaspoon ground turmeric

2 teaspoons besan (gram or chick-pea flour)

300ml (10fl oz) hot semi-skimmed milk

2 tablespoons chopped fresh coriander leaves

• Preheat a small frying pan over medium heat for about 1 minute. Reduce the heat to low and add the coriander seeds, cumin seeds, peppercorns, chillies and sunflower seeds. Roast the spices for 1 minute or until they release their aroma. Transfer to a plate and cool, then grind the spices to a fine powder in a coffee or spice mill.

• Cut the chicken breasts into 5cm (2in) cubes or halve the thighs, and put them in a heavy non-stick saucepan, at least 30cm (12in) in diameter. Add the ginger and garlic purées, the onion, cinnamon, cardamoms and salt. Cook over high heat, stirring, for 5–6 minutes or until the chicken begins to brown.

• Reduce the heat to low-medium, cover the pan and cook for 15 minutes, stirring at least twice. Remove the lid and increase the heat to medium-high, then cook, stirring frequently, until the liquid reduces and thickens to a paste.

- Add the ground spices and turmeric. Cook for a further 2–3 minutes, stirring constantly, until the chicken is well browned.

- Blend the besan with a little water to make a thin paste and strain it through a fine sieve into the milk, pushing through any tiny lumps that form. Stir well, then pour over the chicken and reduce the heat to low. Cover the pan tightly and cook for 15–20 minutes or until the sauce has thickened and the chicken is tender.

- Stir in the coriander leaves and remove from the heat. Serve with Saffron Rice (see page 148), accompanied by a raita or vegetable dish, such as Leeks with Coconut (see page 175).

CHICKEN IN APRICOT JUICE

SERVES 6

Murgh Khubani

Each serving contains
Kcals: 330
g fat: 8
g saturated fat: 3

Preparation time: 20–25 minutes, plus marinating
Cooking time: 35–40 minutes

A gorgeous dish from Kashmir with a sweet, savoury and tangy-hot flavour. Kashmir is noted for its exquisite fruits and flowers and Kashmiri chefs are highly prized throughout the country for their skill and talent in producing fabulous dishes with local produce. Although cooked without fat, this version of a famous chicken dish is every bit as delicious as the original.

6 boneless chicken breasts, about 1kg (2¼lb), skinned

115g (4oz) low-fat plain yogurt

2 teaspoons Ginger Purée (see page 16)

2 teaspoons Garlic Purée (see page 15)

5–6 shallots, finely chopped

1 teaspoon Roasted Ground Cumin (see page 20)

2 teaspoons Roasted Ground Coriander (see page 21)

½–1 teaspoon chilli powder

12 ready-to-eat dried apricots

400ml (14fl oz) hot water

1–2 green chillies, seeded and coarsely chopped

1 teaspoon salt or to taste

½ teaspoon sugar

¼ teaspoon ground cardamom

¼ teaspoon ground nutmeg

90ml (3fl oz) single cream substitute

2 tablespoons chopped fresh coriander leaves

- Cut each chicken breast diagonally into 2–3 chunky pieces. In a large bowl, blend the remaining ingredients up to and including the chilli powder. Add the chicken and mix well, then cover and marinate for 3–4 hours. If you wish, you can leave the chicken to marinate overnight in the refrigerator, but bring it to room temperature before cooking.

- Roughly chop the apricots and soak them in 150ml (5fl oz) of the hot water for 15 minutes, then purée them in a blender with the chillies. Set aside.

- Put the marinated chicken in a non-stick saucepan, at least 30cm (12in) in diameter, and place over medium-high heat. Cook for 3–4 minutes, stirring, until the chicken changes colour and begins to release its juices. Cover the pan, reduce the heat to low and simmer for 15 minutes. Remove the lid and increase the heat to high. Cook for 10–12 minutes or until all the liquid evaporates, reducing the heat to medium towards the last 1–2 minutes.

- Add the apricot purée, salt, sugar and remaining hot water. Mix well, cover and simmer for 6–7 minutes. Add the cardamom and nutmeg and cook, uncovered, for 5 minutes over medium heat. Stir in the cream substitute and coriander leaves and remove from the heat.

- Serve with boiled basmati rice or any bread, accompanied by a dry-spiced vegetable dish, such as Carrots and Green Beans with Poppy Seeds (see page 170).

---

* COOK'S TIP: If the yogurt curdles in step 3, add 2 teaspoons besan (gram or chick-pea flour) blended with a little water.

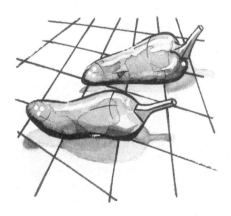

CHICKEN IN COCONUT MILK

SERVES 4

Nariyal ki Murgh

Preparation time: 20–25 minutes
Cooking time: 35–40 minutes

Each serving contains
Kcals: 325
g fat: 12
g saturated fat: 6

Coconut milk enriches a dish, but it is high in saturated fat, so only a small quantity is used in this recipe and when it is divided among four the amount per portion is negligible. You can buy coconut milk powder from all good supermarkets; canned unsweetened coconut milk is an alternative – use 150ml (5fl oz) blended with an equal measure of hot water. The absence of any other added fat gives a light and refreshing result.

900g (2lb) chicken breasts or thighs, skinned

1 large onion, finely chopped

1 tablespoon Garlic Purée (see page 15)

1 tablespoon Ginger Purée (see page 16)

55g (2oz) low-fat plain yogurt

½ teaspoon ground turmeric

2 teaspoons Ground Roasted Coriander (see page 21)

1 teaspoon Ground Roasted Cumin (see page 20)

½–1 teaspoon chilli powder

1 teaspoon salt or to taste

30g (1oz) coconut milk powder

300ml (10fl oz) hot water

4 green chillies, with the stalks intact

8–10 curry leaves

½ teaspoon Garam Masala (see page 22)

1 tablespoon lemon juice

- If using chicken breasts, use poultry scissors or a meat cleaver to chop the joints into two smaller portions. Thighs can be left whole. Put the chicken into a non-stick saucepan, at least 30cm (12in) in diameter, and add the onion, garlic and ginger purées and yogurt. Mix thoroughly then cover the pan. Cook over medium heat, until the contents begin to bubble. Reduce the heat to low and stir the chicken once, then cover and cook for 20 minutes, stirring occasionally.

- Increase the heat to high and cook the chicken, uncovered, until the liquid has reduced and thickened slightly, then reduce the heat to medium. The chicken will have now released its natural fat. Add the turmeric, coriander and cumin, the chilli powder and salt.

- Cook, stirring constantly, until the sauce is reduced to a paste-like consistency and the fat from the chicken is clearly visible – this will take

4–5 minutes.

- Blend the coconut milk powder with the hot water and add to the chicken with the fresh chillies, curry leaves and garam masala. Simmer, uncovered, for 6–8 minutes. Sir in the lemon juice and remove from the heat.

- Serve immediately, with boiled basmati rice and Spinach Raita (see page 182) or Cauliflower with Green Chutney (see page 172).

---

* COOK'S TIP: The chicken is left on the bone for extra flavour. If you want to cook boneless meat, then add 225g (8oz) bones to the pan and remove them before serving the dish. Alternatively, use Aromatic Stock (see page 23).

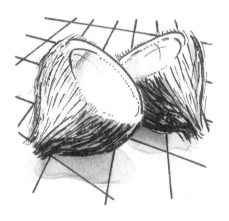

CHICKEN WITH CHILLI AND LIME

SERVES 4

Mirchi aur Nimbuwali Murgh

Each serving contains
Kcals: 196
g fat: 7
g saturated fat: 2.25

Preparation time: 20 minutes
Cooking time: 30 minutes

This dish has an attractive, fresh appearance with an aroma and flavour to match. Chilli and lime is a combination which is hard to beat. Do not be alarmed by the quantity and variety of chilli used here – the powdered chilli complements the tart limes and the fresh chillies are seeded to reduce their pungency. You can further reduce their hot flavour by soaking the slit chillies in cold water for 15–20 minutes, then rinsing them well.

500g (1lb 2oz) boneless chicken thighs, skinned and halved

juice of 2 limes

2 teaspoons Ginger Purée (see page 16)

2 teaspoons Garlic Purée (see page15)

1 large onion, finely chopped

½ teaspoon ground turmeric

1 teaspoon Ground Roasted Cumin (see page 20)

2 teaspoons Ground Roasted Coriander (see page 21)

½–1 teaspoon chilli powder

1 teaspoon salt or to taste

1½ teaspoons sugar

225g (8oz) Boiled Onion Purée (see page 17)

200ml (7fl oz) warm water

2 tablespoons chopped fresh coriander leaves

1–2 green chillies, seeded and cut into julienne strips

2 red chillies, seeded and cut into julienne strips

½ teaspoon Garam Masala (see page 22)

- Put the chicken into a non-stick saucepan, at least 25cm (10in) in diameter, and add the lime juice, ginger and garlic purées, chopped onion and turmeric. Stir to mix thoroughly. Place the pan over medium heat and cook gently until the contents begin to bubble, then cover and cook for 10–12 minutes over medium-low heat, stirring occasionally. At the end of this time, the chicken will have released its juices.

- Remove the lid and increase the heat slightly. Cook the chicken until the juices are reduced to a thick paste – this will take 4–5 minutes. Stir frequently to ensure that the thickened paste does not stick to the bottom of the pan.

- Add the cumin, ground coriander, chilli powder, salt and sugar. Reduce the heat to medium and continue to cook for a further 1–2 minutes, stirring constantly.

- Add half the onion purée and cook, stirring frequently, for 3–4 minutes or until the onion purée is dry enough to coat the pieces of chicken. Repeat with the remaining onion purée and warm water, then cook, uncovered, for 4–5 minutes or until the sauce has thickened.

- Reserve a little of the fresh coriander and each variety of chillies for garnish and add the remainder to the chicken along with the garam masala. Stir well to distribute the ingredients and remove the pan from the heat. Garnish with the reserved coriander and chillies, and serve with Tandoori Bread (see page 162) or Chapatis (see page 159) and Cucumber and Peanut Salad (see page 188).

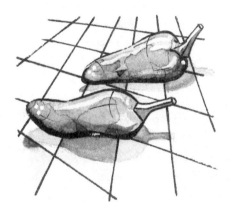

CHICKEN KORMA

SERVES 4

Murgh Korma

Preparation time: 15–20 minutes
Cooking time: 35 minutes

Each serving contains
Kcals: 280
g fat: 10
g saturated fat: 3

In the West, korma has come to represent a dish which is very mild and drowned in cream, but, authentically, it is the Indian term for braising. A korma can be mild or rather fiery, depending on regional variations; for example, in the south a korma is enriched with coconut milk and plenty of chillies are added to counteract the sweetness. Korma is Mogul in origin and, in the north, where the Moguls established themselves, there are many versions of this popular dish, usually with rich ingredients like saffron, nuts, khoya (full-fat dried milk) and cream. This recipe is a healthy variation on a northern korma.

30g (1oz) unroasted cashew nut pieces

pinch of saffron threads

75ml (2½fl oz) boiling water

675g (1½lb) boneless chicken breasts or thighs, skinned

75g (2½oz) low-fat plain yogurt

1 large onion, finely chopped

6 green cardamom pods, bruised

2 x 2.5cm (1in) pieces of cinnamon stick

4 cloves

1 tablespoon Ginger Purée (see page 16)

1 tablespoon Garlic Purée (see page 15)

1 teaspoon salt or to taste

½ teaspoon ground turmeric

½–1 teaspoon chilli powder

½ teaspoon ground white pepper

1 tablespoon Ground Roasted Coriander (see page 21)

300ml (10fl oz) Aromatic Stock (see page 23)

115g (4oz) Browned Onion Purée (see page 19)

2 tablespoons single cream substitute

½ teaspoon Garam Masala (see page 22)

1 tablespoon low-fat fromage frais

½ teaspoon paprika

- Put the cashews and saffron in a bowl and pour in the boiling water. Leave to soak for 15–20 minutes.

- Meanwhile, cut the chicken breasts into 5cm (2in) cubes or halve the thighs. Put the chicken in a non-stick saucepan, at least 25cm (10 in) in diameter. Add the yogurt, chopped onion, cardamoms, cinnamon, cloves and ginger and garlic purées. Mix thoroughly and place over medium heat, then cover and cook for 5–6 minutes.

- Stir the chicken, reduce the heat to low and cook, covered, for a further 5–7 minutes. Remove the lid and increase the heat to medium-high, then cook, stirring frequently, for 6–8 minutes or until the liquid evaporates to form a thick paste.

- Add the salt, turmeric, chilli powder, pepper and coriander, and cook, stirring frequently, for 3–4 minutes or until the chicken begins to brown. Stir in the stock and onion purée. Cover and cook over low heat for 8–10 minutes.

- Meanwhile, purée the cashews, saffron and their soaking water in a blender. Add the cream substitute and process until smooth. Pour this over the chicken. Add the garam masala and cook, uncovered, for 2–3 minutes.

- Transfer the korma to a serving dish. Swirl the fromage frais over the top and sprinkle with the paprika. Serve immediately, with Saffron Rice (see page 148) and Carrots and Green Beans with Poppy Seeds (see page 170).

---

* **COOK'S TIP: If you do not have time to make the stock, add 225g (8oz) chicken bones and remove them before serving the dish.**

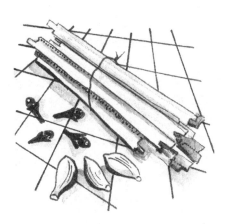

CHICKEN IN LENTIL SAUCE

SERVES 4

Murgh Dhansak

Preparation time: 25 minutes, plus soaking
Cooking time: 1 hour 15 minutes

Each serving contains
Kcals: 355
g fat: 10
g saturated fat: 3

In the thirteenth century a group of Persians fled their country to avoid religious persecution and they landed on the West Coast of India, now the state of Gujarat, and contributed their culinary influence to the diverse cooking of India. For dhansak, probably the best-loved dish from Western India, the meat is always cooked with lentils and vegetables. Dhan means rice and sak is vegetables, and Fried Brown Rice (see page 149) is the traditional accompaniment.

Dhal

55g (2oz) masoor dhal (red lentils)

55g (2oz) toor dhal (yellow split lentils, see page 9)

55g (2oz) moong dhal (skinless split mung beans, see page 8)

1 small aubergine, about 225g (8oz)

½ teaspoon ground turmeric

1–2 green chillies, seeded and chopped

5cm (2in) piece of cinnamon stick, halved

½ teaspoon salt or to taste

Spice mix

1 tablespoon coriander seeds

1½ teaspoons cumin seeds

2.5cm (1 in) piece of cinnamon stick, halved

10–12 black peppercorns

seeds from 1 brown and 6 green cardamom pods

1–2 dried red chillies, chopped

Chicken

8 boneless chicken thighs, skinned and halved

55g (2oz) low-fat plain yogurt

2 teaspoons Ginger Purée (see page 16)

2 teaspoons Garlic Purée (see page 15)

½ teaspoon ground turmeric

1 teaspoon paprika

1 large onion, finely chopped

170g (6oz) tomatoes, chopped

1 teaspoon dried fenugreek leaves

1 teaspoon salt or to taste

1 teaspoon sugar

75ml (2½fl oz) warm water

1½ tablespoons tamarind juice

2–3 tablespoons chopped fresh coriander leaves

- Wash the masoor dhal, toor dhal and moong dhal in cold water until the water runs clear, then place in a bowl, cover with plenty of cold water and soak for 30 minutes.

- Meanwhile, quarter the aubergine lengthways and cut into 5cm (2in) pieces. Halve the wider ends, if necessary, before cutting them into pieces. Place in a bowl, cover with cold water to prevent discoloration and leave to soak until required.

- Prepare the spice mix. Preheat a small frying pan over medium heat. Add all the spices, except the chillies, then reduce the heat to low and stir for about 1 minute, until the spices release their aroma. Turn off the heat and add the chillies. Stir for 30 seconds, then transfer the spices to a plate and cool slightly before grinding to a fine powder in a coffee or spice mill. Set aside.

- Drain the lentils and aubergine and place in a saucepan. Add 600ml (1 pint) water and bring to the boil. Reduce the heat to medium, add the turmeric, chillies and cinnamon stick, and cook, uncovered, for 5–6 minutes. Reduce the heat to low, cover the pan and simmer for 25 minutes, stirring occasionally.

- Add the salt to the dhal, then set aside to cool until just hot. Discard the cinnamon and purée the dhal in a blender or press it through a sieve. Set aside.

- Put the chicken in a non-stick saucepan and add the yogurt, ginger and garlic purées, turmeric, paprika and onion. Place over a high heat and stir until the chicken begins to sizzle. Cook for 4–5 minutes, stirring frequently.

- Reduce the heat to low, cover the pan and cook for 10 minutes. Remove the lid and cook, stirring frequently, for 6–7 minutes over medium-high heat until most of the liquid has evaporated.

- Reduce the heat to low. Add the ground spices and cook for 2–3 minutes, stirring. Stir in the tomatoes, fenugreek leaves, salt and sugar, and cook for a further 2–3 minutes.

- Pour the cooked lentil sauce and water into the chicken. Reduce the heat to low, cover the pan and cook for 15 minutes or until the chicken is tender. Stir regularly to ensure that the thickened sauce does not stick to the pan, adding a little extra water if necessary.

- Stir in the tamarind juice and coriander leaves, then serve with Fried Brown Rice (see page 149)

CHICKEN DO-PIAZA

Do-Piaza Murgh

Preparation time: 20 minutes
Cooking time: 30 minutes

Each serving contains
Kcals: 244
g fat: 9
g saturated fat: 3

The meaning of the word do-piaza *remains controversial:* do *means two or twice and* piaz *is onion. Therefore, some believe the name refers to the amount of onions used in the recipe (twice the norm), while others insist that the name comes from the equal quantities of onions and meat which were used in the original recipe. The third and more reasonable explanation is that the dish was named after the Mogul Emperor Akbar's courtier, Mullah Dopiaza.*

8 boneless chicken thighs, skinned and halved

2 teaspoons Ginger Purée (see page 16)

2 teaspoons Garlic Purée (see page 15)

2 x 5cm (2in) pieces of cinnamon stick, halved

2 brown cardamom pods, bruised

4 cloves

2 bay leaves, crumpled

1 large red onion, halved and finely sliced

½ teaspoon ground turmeric

½–1 teaspoon chilli powder

1 teaspoon Ground Roasted Cumin (see page 20)

1 teaspoon Ground Roasted Coriander (see page 21)

2 tablespoons low-fat plain yogurt

225g (8oz) Boiled Onion Purée (see page 17)

1 teaspoon salt or to taste

1 tablespoon tomato purée

300ml (10fl oz) Aromatic Stock (see page 23)

1 large tomato, cut into chunks

2–4 green chillies, with the stalks intact

2–3 tablespoons chopped fresh coriander leaves

- Put the chicken in a heavy non-stick saucepan, at least 30cm (12in) in diameter, and add the ginger and garlic purées, cinnamon, cardamoms, cloves and bay leaves. Cook over medium-high heat for 7–8 minutes, stirring, until the chicken begins to brown.

- Reduce the heat slightly, add the red onion and continue to cook for 3–4 minutes, stirring frequently.

- Add the turmeric, chilli powder, cumin and coriander, and cook for

80 *Fat Free Indian Cookery*

1 minute. Add half the yogurt and cook for 2–3 minutes, then repeat with the remaining yogurt. Add the onion purée and continue to cook for 3–4 minutes, stirring.

● Stir in the salt, tomato purée and stock, and bring to the boil. Reduce the heat to low and cook, uncovered, for 12–15 minutes. Stir occasionally to ensure that the thickened sauce does not stick to the pan.

● Add the tomato, chillies and fresh coriander. Cook for 1 minute, then serve with Tandoori Bread (see page 162) and a raita.

---

* **COOK'S TIP: Do not remove the stalks from the green chillies unless you like your food hot. Once the stalk is removed, the chilli will release its juices into the sauce, making it hot.**

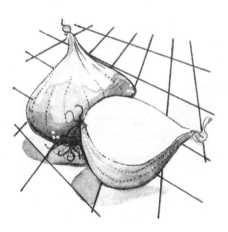

CHILLI CHICKEN

Murgh aur Mirchi

Preparation time: 20 minutes, plus marinating
Cooking time: 25–30 minutes

Each serving contains
Kcals: 240
g fat: 9
g saturated fat: 3

This is a fairly dry dish, cooked by the bhuna method, which is a form of stir-frying. When finished, the sauce is reduced to a thick paste which coats the chicken. Strips of red and green chilli, and coarse-cut coriander leaves make the chicken look irresistibly yummy, and it tastes delicious with any bread and a chutney or raita.

8 boneless chicken thighs, skinned and halved

2 tablespoons lemon juice

1 teaspoon salt or to taste

2 teaspoons Ginger Purée (see page 16)

2 teaspoons Garlic Purée (see page 15)

½ teaspoon ground turmeric

½–1 teaspoon chilli powder

1 teaspoon Ground Roasted Coriander (see page 21)

1 teaspoon Ground Roasted Cumin (see page 20)

280g (10oz) Browned Onion Purée (see page 19)

1½ teaspoons sugar

225g (8oz) tomatoes, finely chopped

75ml (2½fl oz) warm water

1–2 red chillies, seeded and cut into julienne strips

1–2 green chillies, seeded and cut into julienne strips

½ teaspoon Garam Masala (see page 22)

2–3 tablespoons coarsely chopped fresh coriander leaves

- Put the chicken in a large bowl and rub the lemon juice and salt into the pieces. Set aside for 30 minutes.

- Put the chicken in a non-stick saucepan, at least 30cm (12in) in diameter and add the ginger and garlic purées. Cook over medium heat, stirring, until sizzling. Increase the heat to high and cook for 2–3 minutes, stirring constantly.

- Add the turmeric, chilli powder, ground coriander and cumin, and reduce the heat to medium. Cook for 2 minutes, stirring constantly.

- Stir in half the onion purée and cook for 4–5 minutes, stirring occasionally, then add the remaining onion purée and sugar. Continue to cook for a further 4–5 minutes, stirring frequently.

- Add the tomatoes and the water, mix well and cover the pan tightly.

82 *Fat Free Indian Cookery*

- Reduce the heat to low and cook for 10 minutes.

- Remove the lid and increase the heat to medium. Continue to cook for 3–4 minutes, stirring frequently, then add the red and green chillies and garam masala. Cook for 4–5 minutes or until the sauce has thickened.

- Finally, stir in the coriander leaves and cook for 1 minute. Remove from the heat and serve immediately.

---

* **COOK'S TIP: Removing the seeds from the chillies will reduce their pungency. If you want to reduce the heat further, soak the strips in cold water until required. Drain well before adding to the dish.**

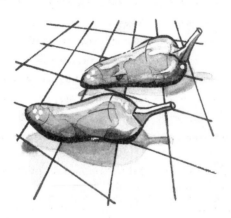

DRY-SPICED CHICKEN DRUMSTICKS

Sukha Masaleki Tangri

Preparation time: 15 minutes
Cooking time: 25 minutes

Each serving contains
Kcals: 215
g fat: 9
g saturated fat: 3

Here, a simple cooking method contributes fabulous aroma and taste to a dish that makes a good mid-week family meal or can be served as a side dish on a dinner-party menu.

8 chicken drumsticks, skinned

2 teaspoons Garlic Purée (see page 15)

2 teaspoons Ginger Purée (see page 16)

½–1 teaspoon salt or to taste

55g (2oz) low-fat plain yogurt

2 teaspoons Ground Roasted Coriander (see page 21)

1 teaspoons Ground Roasted Cumin (see page 20)

½–1 teaspoon chilli powder

½ teaspoon ground turmeric

300ml (10fl oz) warm water

1 teaspoon Garam Masala (see page 22)

85g (3oz) canned chopped tomatoes, with their juice

2 tablespoons chopped fresh coriander leaves

1 tablespoon chopped fresh mint or ½ teaspoon dried mint

- Put the chicken drumsticks in a non-stick saucepan, at least 30cm (12in) in diameter, and add the garlic and ginger purées, salt, yogurt, ground coriander, cumin, chilli powder, turmeric and water. Bring to the boil over medium heat. Cover and reduce the heat to low. Cook for 20 minutes, stirring occasionally.

- Remove the lid and increase the heat to high. Cook the drumsticks for 2–3 minutes or until the sauce thickens slightly, stirring frequently.

- Reduce the heat to medium. Add the garam masala, tomatoes, fresh coriander and mint. Stir and cook until the sauce resembles a thick paste. Remove from the heat and serve with soft, puffy Chapatis (see page 159) and a raita or Spiced Sweet Potatoes (see page 167).

---

* **COOK'S TIP: For a cook-ahead meal, cook to the end of step 1, then cool and chill overnight or for up to 2 days. Complete the cooking process just before serving.**

84 *Fat Free Indian Cookery*

CHICKEN IN GREEN SAUCE

SERVES 4

Hariyali Murgh

Each serving contains
Kcals: 225
g fat: 9
g saturated fat: 3

Preparation time: 15 minutes
Cooking time: 25–30 minutes

This is a super, quick dish with fabulous flavour. The chicken is cooked in a green spice paste without added stock or water. Traditionally, ghee or oil is added to fry the chicken at the end of the cooking time, but this light version is delicious without the added fat.

30g (1oz) fresh coriander leaves and stalks, coarsely chopped

15–20 fresh mint leaves

4 large garlic cloves, chopped

2.5cm (1in) cube of fresh root ginger, peeled and coarsely chopped

1–2 green chillies, seeded and chopped

1 onion, coarsely chopped

2 tomatoes, about 125g (4½oz) in total, skinned and chopped

55g (2oz) low-fat plain yogurt

½ teaspoon chilli powder

2 teaspoons Ground Roasted Coriander (see page 21)

4 green cardamom pods, bruised

8 boneless chicken thighs, skinned and halved
or 675g (1½lb) boneless chicken breasts, skinned and cut into 5cm (2in) cubes

1 teaspoon salt or to taste

- Purée the coriander, mint, garlic, ginger, chillies, onion, tomatoes and yogurt in a blender. Pour into a non-stick saucepan, at least 30cm (12in) in diameter.

- Add the remaining ingredients, except the salt, and place the pan over high heat. Cook, stirring, for 4–5 minutes or until the chicken turns opaque. Reduce the heat to low, cover the pan and cook for 20–25 minutes.

- Stir in the salt and cook, uncovered, over medium heat for 8–10 minutes or until the sauce has reduced and resembles a thick paste.

- Serve with Tandoori Bread (see page 162) and Mixed Vegetable Curry (see page 173) or a Raita.

CHICKEN MEATBALLS IN A RICH SAUCE

Murgh Kofta Shahi

Preparation time: 35 minutes, plus chilling
Cooking time: 35 minutes

Each serving contains
Kcals: 334
g fat: 18
g saturated fat: 6.5

These melt-in-the-mouth chicken meatballs are simmered in a korma sauce enriched with cashew nut purée. The dish is equally delicious made with minced turkey.

Meatballs

450g (1lb) minced chicken

1 teaspoon Garam Masala (see page 22)

1 large egg

1–2 green chillies, seeded and coarsely chopped

10g (¼oz) fresh coriander leaves and stalks

2 large garlic cloves, coarsely chopped

2.5cm (1in) cube of fresh root ginger, peeled and coarsely chopped

1 small onion, coarsely chopped

½ teaspoon salt or to taste

Sauce

55g (2oz) unroasted cashew nut pieces

450ml (15fl oz) hot water

1 tablespoon besan (gram or chick-pea flour)

85g (3oz) low-fat plain yogurt

½–1 teaspoon chilli powder

½ teaspoon ground turmeric

1 teaspoon paprika

1 teaspoon Ground Roasted Cumin (see page 20)

1 teaspoon Ground Roasted Coriander (see page 21)

1 tablespoon tomato purée

1 teaspoon salt or to taste

1 teaspoon sugar

4 green cardamom pods, bruised

5cm (2in) piece of cinnamon stick, halved

½ teaspoon Garam Masala (see page 22)

150ml (5fl oz) single cream substitute

2 tablespoons chopped fresh coriander leaves

- Put all the ingredients for the meatballs in a food processor and blend until smooth. Transfer to a mixing bowl and cover with cling film, then chill for 30 minutes. If you do not have a food processor, finely chop the chillies, coriander, garlic, ginger and onion (or purée these ingredients in a blender) and mix with the other ingredients by hand until thoroughly combined.

- Meanwhile, for the sauce, soak the cashew nuts in 150ml (5fl oz) of the hot water for 20 minutes.

- Shape the kofta mixture into 16 balls, each about the size of a lime, smoothing them by gently rotating and pressing between the palms of your hands.

- To make the sauce, sieve the besan and blend it to a smooth paste with a little cold water, then mix in the yogurt, chilli powder, turmeric, paprika, cumin, ground coriander, tomato purée, salt and sugar. Set aside.

- Use a saucepan large enough to hold the meatballs in a single layer and add the remaining hot water, cardamoms and cinnamon stick. Heat until simmering, then carefully add the meatballs in a single layer. Cover and cook for 10–12 minutes or until the meatballs are firm enough for the liquid to be stirred.

- Reduce the heat to low and carefully stir in the besan and spice mixture. Re-cover the pan and cook for 10 minutes.

- Meanwhile, purée the cashew nuts with the water in which they were soaked and add to the meatballs with the garam masala and cream substitute. Simmer for 5–7 minutes.

- Stir in the coriander leaves and serve immediately. Any bread or boiled basmati rice makes a suitable accompaniment with a vegetable dish, such as Cabbage with Ginger (see page 169).

---

* **COOK'S TIP: For puréed cashews, buy broken nuts or cashew pieces as they are less expensive.**

CHICKEN IN TOMATO AND COCONUT SAUCE

SERVES 4

Tamatar aur Nariyal ki Murgh

Preparation time: 15 minutes
Cooking time: 35 minutes

Each serving contains
Kcals: 260
g fat: 14
g saturated fat: 7

When you are absolutely frantic, this recipe will rescue you time and time again. You simply mix everything together and while the chicken is cooking, boil the rice. There will still be time to make a salad.

30g (1oz) desiccated coconut

150ml (5fl oz) boiling water

15g (½oz) fresh coriander leaves and stalks

1–2 green chillies, seeded

2 large garlic cloves

2.5cm (1in) cube of fresh root ginger, peeled and coarsely chopped

225g (8oz) passata

8 chicken thighs, skinned

1 teaspoon salt or to taste

2 tablespoons single cream substitute

- Soak the coconut in the hot water for 10–15 minutes. Purée the coconut and its soaking water in a blender with the coriander, chillies, garlic and ginger until smooth.

- Put the passata, chicken and salt in a saucepan, at least 30cm (12in) in diameter, and place over medium heat. When the passata begins to bubble, reduce the heat to low, cover and cook for 20 minutes.

- Stir in the blended coconut mixture and heat until the sauce begins to bubble again, then cover the pan and cook for 10–12 minutes.

- Finally, add the cream substitute, cook for 1 minute and serve at once.

---

* **COOK'S TIP: Passata is a thick sieved tomato purée. Alternatively, use the same amount of canned tomatoes and purée them in a blender or sieve them until smooth.**

CHICKEN TIKKA MASALA

SERVES 4

Murgh Tikka Masala

Each serving contains
Kcals: 445
g fat: 22
g saturated fat: 10

Preparation time: 5 minutes, plus preparing chicken tikka
Cooking time: 17–18 minutes, plus cooking chicken tikka

Chicken tikka is a traditional Indian dish, but masala is a clever invention. In the seventies a masala (spiced) sauce was added to chicken tikka to satisfy a customer who thought the meat was too dry. Now, there is hardly any Indian restaurant in Britain that does not have CTM (as it is known in the trade!) as one of the most popular dishes on the menu. I have even come across this dish in some restaurants in India.

150ml (5fl oz) single cream substitute

55g (2oz) half-fat crème fraîche

250ml (8½fl oz) Aromatic Stock (see page 23)

½ teaspoon Ground Roasted Cumin (see page 20)

½ teaspoon Ground Roasted Coriander (see page 21)

1–2 green chillies, seeded and chopped

1 tablespoon tomato purée

½ teaspoon salt or to taste

½ teaspoon sugar

1 quantity cooked Chicken Tikka (see page 34)

2 tablespoons finely chopped fresh coriander leaves

- Mix all the ingredients, except the cooked chicken tikka and coriander leaves, in a saucepan and place over medium heat. As soon as the sauce starts bubbling, turn the heat down to low and simmer for 10 minutes.

- Cool the sauce slightly, then purée it in a blender or press it through a sieve. Return to the saucepan and add the cooked chicken tikka. Simmer for 5 minutes or until the chicken is thoroughly heated.

- Add the coriander leaves and simmer for 2–3 minutes. Serve with Tandoori Bread (see page 162) or Cumin-Coriander Rice (see page 146) and a raita.

COOK'S TIP: The chicken tikka can be cooked in advance, cooled and chilled or frozen with all its cooking juices. Thaw the chicken and, for extra flavour, be sure to add the juices to the sauce at the start of cooking the above recipe.

BAKED CHICKEN

Dum ka Murgh

Each serving contains
Kcals: 210
g fat: 9
g saturated fat: 2

Preparation time: 30 minutes, plus marinating
Cooking time: 45 minutes

This is an adaptation of a recipe from Hyderabad, a princely city with forts and palaces in southern India. The last of the Mogul Emperors retired to this city, and the strong tradition of Mogul cooking makes the cuisine of Hyderabad unique among the southern states.

4 chicken joints, skinned

1 tablespoon lemon juice

1 teaspoon salt or to taste

½ teaspoon chilli powder

125g (4½oz) low-fat plain yogurt

5cm (2in) cube of fresh root ginger, peeled and coarsely chopped

4 garlic cloves, peeled and coarsely chopped

5–6 shallots, coarsely chopped

2 teaspoons white poppy seeds

1 tablespoon sunflower seeds

seeds from 4 green cardamom pods

2 cloves

2.5cm (1in) piece of cinnamon stick, broken

Basting sauce

pinch of saffron threads, pounded

2 tablespoons hot milk

1 tablespoon finely chopped fresh coriander leaves

½ teaspoon dried mint

- Prick the chicken joints all over with the point of a sharp knife or a fork. Rub the lemon juice, salt and chilli powder into the chicken and set aside.

- Place the yogurt in a blender and add the ginger, garlic and shallots. Purée until smooth.

- In a coffee or spice mill, grind the poppy seeds, sunflower seeds, cardamom seeds, cloves and cinnamon to a fine powder.

- Mix the ground spices and yogurt purée, then pour over the chicken joints. Turn the joints and spoon the mixture over them until they are thoroughly coated. Cover and leave to marinate for 3–4 hours in a cool place or overnight in the refrigerator. Bring the chicken to room temperature before cooking.

- For the basting sauce, soak the saffron threads in the hot milk for 15 minutes, then stir in the coriander and mint. Preheat the oven to 200°C/400°F/Gas 6.

- Line a roasting tin with foil and brush it lightly with oil. Place the chicken and marinade in the tin and bake for 15–20 minutes. Turn the joints over and bake for a further 15–20 minutes, basting with the pan juices at least twice.

- Brush some of the basting sauce over the chicken and continue to cook for 3–4 minutes. Turn the joints over and brush with the remaining basting sauce. Cook for a final 2–3 minutes. Serve immediately, with a raita and Chapatis (see page 159) or Karnataka Potato Curry (see page 166).

SPICY ROAST CHICKEN

Masala Tandoori Murgh

Each serving contains
Kcals: 215
g fat: 6
g saturated fat: 2

Preparation time: 25 minutes, plus marinating
Cooking time: 45–50 minutes.

Although similar, this is not quite the same as tandoori chicken. In Indian cooking, a tandoor (clay oven) is used for roasting and it imparts its characteristic flavour to the food. In this recipe, I have modified the process and cooked the chicken in a hot oven. I am delighted with the result because it captures the tandoori flavour as closely as possible. For a special Sunday lunch, serve Vegetable Pilau (see page 158) or Savoury Potato Mash (see page 165) and Kohlrabi Salad (see page 189) as accompaniments.

1 roasting chicken, about 1.35kg (3lb)

85g (3oz) low-fat plain yogurt

1 tablespoon lemon juice

1 tablespoon Garlic Purée (see page 15)

1 tablespoon Ginger Purée (see page 16)

½–1 teaspoon chilli powder

½–1 teaspoon salt or to taste

1 teaspoon Ground Roasted Cumin (see page 20)

1 teaspoon Ground Roasted Coriander (see page 21)

Garnish

sprigs of fresh coriander

1–2 red chillies, seeded and sliced

red onion slices

- Skin the chicken: the easiest way to do this is to hold the chicken with one hand and cover the other hand with a clean tea-towel or new disposable dishcloth, then start pulling the skin away from the neck end. Carefully work your way around the thighs and legs right down to the stomach end of the chicken. The cloth prevents slipping and is much easier and quicker than using a knife.

- Lay the chicken on a flat surface and make short, deep incisions all over the flesh, including the wings, inside thighs, legs and back. Remove the parson's nose and wing and leg tips.

- Mix all the remaining ingredients, except the cumin and coriander. Rub the mixture well into the chicken, making sure you work the mixture into the incisions. Place the chicken in a deep container, cover and chill overnight. Bring the chicken to room temperature before cooking.

- Preheat the oven to 200°C/400°F/Gas 6. Place the marinated chicken in a 30 x 20cm (12 x 8in) roasting tin. Spread any remaining marinade on the chicken and roast for 25 minutes.

- Pour 90ml (3fl oz) water into the roasting tin and continue to cook for a further 20 minutes. Baste the chicken generously with the cooking juices, then cook for a further 15–20 minutes, basting twice.

- Sprinkle the cumin and ground coriander all over the chicken and cook for a final 5 minutes. Baste again with the thickened cooking juices so that the spices cling to the chicken. Transfer to a serving dish.

- Strain any remaining cooking juices and pour them over the chicken. Garnish with sprigs of coriander, sliced chillies and onion slicess, and serve immediately.

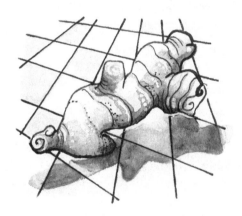

SEMI-TANDOORI CHICKEN

Adha Tandoori Murgh

**Preparation time: 15 minutes, plus marinating
Cooking time: 25 minutes**

Each serving contains
Kcals: 180
g fat: 4.5
g saturated fat: 1.5

*I christened this dish semi-tandoori as I have used only half the range of spices that
are used in classic tandoori chicken. It is a simple recipe, but it has a spectacular
taste and appearance, and is simply divine served with Chapatis (see page 159),
Savoury Potato Mash (see page 165) and Mixed Vegetable Curry (see page 173)
with a raita or chutney. Use either chicken leg or breast quarters, or a combination
of the two.*

4 chicken joints, skinned

150g (5½oz) low-fat plain yogurt

½–1 teaspoon chilli powder

½ teaspoon ground turmeric

1 tablespoon Garlic Purée (see page 15)

1 tablespoon Ginger Purée (see page 16)

½ teaspoon salt or to taste

2 teaspoons cumin seeds

2 tablespoons chopped fresh coriander leaves

● Score both sides of the chicken joints with a sharp knife and put them in a
large bowl. Mix all the remaining ingredients, except the cumin seeds and
coriander leaves, and rub this mixture into the chicken. Cover and leave to
marinate for 3–4 hours or overnight in the refrigerator. Bring the chicken
to room temperature before cooking it.

● Preheat the grill to high and line a grill pan (without the rack) with foil.
Lightly brush the foil with oil and place the chicken joints on it. Cook
about 12cm (5in) away from the heat source for 5 minutes.

● Turn the chicken joints over and cook for a further 5 minutes. Turn them
again and reduce the heat to medium, then cook for a further 7–8 minutes
on each side.

● Meanwhile, preheat a small frying pan over medium heat. Add the cumin
seeds and turn off the heat. Stir for 30–60 seconds or until the seeds
release their aroma, then transfer them to a plate and cool slightly. Crush
the seeds in a mortar with a pestle, or on a board using the back of a
wooden spoon.

● Sprinkle the crushed cumin seeds on both sides of the chicken joints and
transfer them to a serving plate. Mix the coriander leaves with the cooking
juices left on the foil, which should be rather like a paste. Spread the paste
evenly over the chicken joints and serve immediately.

TURKEY IN ORANGE JUICE

Turkey Narangi

SERVES 4

Each serving contains
Kcals: 270
g fat: 7
g saturated fat: 2

Preparation time: 20 minutes
Cooking time: 30–35 minutes

This is a light and aromatic dish. As turkey breast meat is virtually fat-free, I have used a little oil here to help develop the flavours of the spices.

1 tablespoon sunflower or soya oil

3 green cardamom pods, bruised

2 x 2.5cm (1in) pieces of cinnamon stick

2 teaspoons Ginger Purée (see page 16)

2 teaspoons Garlic Purée (see page 15)

675g (1½lb) turkey breast fillets, skinned and cut into 2.5cm (1in) cubes

125g (4½oz) low-fat plain yogurt

½ teaspoon ground turmeric

¼–½ teaspoon chilli powder

1 tablespoon Ground Roasted Coriander (see page 21)

1 teaspoon Ground Roasted Cumin (see page 20)

225g (8oz) Boiled Onion Purée (see page 17)

240ml (8fl oz) freshly squeezed orange juice

1 teaspoon salt or to taste

1 teaspoon sugar

1–2 green chillies, seeded and cut into julienne strips

2 tablespoons chopped fresh coriander leaves

- Heat the oil in a non-stick saucepan over low heat and add the cardamoms and cinnamon. Stir the spices for 15–20 seconds. Add the ginger and garlic purées, and fry for 2 minutes, stirring constantly.

- Add the turkey and increase the heat to medium-high. Cook, stirring frequently, for 3–4 minutes or until the turkey is opaque.

- Add the yogurt, turmeric, chilli powder, ground coriander and cumin. Cook for 3–4 minutes, stirring frequently, then increase the heat to high. Continue to cook, stirring frequently, for 5–6 minutes or until all the cooking juices have evaporated and the turkey begins to brown.

- Add the onion purée and cook for 3–4 minutes, then strain the orange juice over the turkey. Add the salt and sugar and bring to the boil. Cover and simmer for 15–20 minutes or until the turkey is tender.

- Add the chillies and coriander. Cook for 1–2 minutes. Serve with rice and Spiced Sweet Potatoes (see page 167) or Cabbage with Ginger (see page 169).

Lamb
Specialities

Lamb is the fattiest of meats and the fat it contains is saturated, therefore I have restricted the number of recipes in this section. The exact fat content depends on various factors, such as the age of the animal, the breed and the cut of meat. The choice of cut is one area over which we can exercise discretion and it is important to select lean joints or cuts to minimize the fat. I have used leg meat in the majority of these recipes as it is the leanest cut. On a positive note, remember that, as well as being high in protein, lamb is a rich source of all the B vitamins, which maintain a healthy nervous system; zinc, necessary for healthy growth; and iron, to prevent anaemia.

Always trim off all visible fat before cutting or preparing the meat. Make sure you cook it slowly and gently as high temperatures toughen meat. In spite of the fact that there is no added fat in any of the recipes (which makes them lower in calories) they are all full of flavour.

All the dishes freeze well. Thaw them in the refrigerator before reheating slowly over gentle heat, adding a little warm water as and when necessary, if sauces begin to dry up.

Make sure the food is piping hot throughout before serving. To freeze dry dishes, such as the Marinated Leg of Lamb (see page 106) or Marinated Lamb Chops (see page 99), cook to the stage where basting is required, then cool and freeze the meat and the cooking juices separately. Thaw completely before finishing the cooking process just before serving.

MARINATED LAMB CHOPS

Tabak Maaz

Preparation time: 10–15 minutes
Cooking time: 35–40 minutes

SERVES 4

Each serving contains
Kcals: 175
g fat: 9
g saturated fat: 4.5

This is an adaptation of a much-loved recipe from the beautiful valley of Kashmir.

4 lamb chump chops or 8 lamb cutlets

300ml (10fl oz) semi-skimmed milk

2 teaspoons Ginger Purée (see page 16)

½ teaspoon freshly ground black pepper

pinch of saffron threads, pounded

1½ teaspoons ground fennel seeds

1½ teaspoons ground cumin

½ teaspoon chilli powder

4 cloves

5cm (2in) piece of cinnamon stick, halved

4 green cardamom pods, bruised

1 teaspoon salt or to taste

½ teaspoon Garam Masala (see page 22)

1 tablespoon chopped fresh mint or ½ teaspoon dried mint

1 tablespoon finely chopped fresh coriander leaves

- Remove the rind and excess fat from the chops or cutlets. Bring a saucepan of water to the boil and add the chops. Bring back to the boil and cook for 2–3 minutes, then drain and rinse the meat.

- Put the drained chops or cutlets into a non-stick saucepan, about 30cm (12in) in diameter, and add the remaining ingredients, except the garam masala, mint and fresh coriander. Place the saucepan over medium heat and stir until the milk begins to bubble. Reduce the heat to low, cover the pan and cook for 30 minutes. Turn the chops over occasionally during cooking.

- Remove the saucepan from the heat and lift out each chop or cutlet with a pair of tongs or a draining spoon and fork. Shake off the cooking liquid back into the pan and set the meat aside on a plate. Strain the cooking liquid and return it to the saucepan with the chops or cutlets.

- Cook over medium heat for 3–4 minutes, turning the chops or cutlets frequently, until the stock has reduced to half its original quantity.

- Add the garam masala, mint and coriander evenly over the chops and continue to cook for 4–5 minutes, turning as before, until the stock evaporates and the chops are browned. Serve with Chapatis (see page 159) and Almond Chutney (see page 183) or Fruit Raita (see page 179).

STIR-FRIED SPICED LAMB

SERVES 4

Bhuna Gosht

Preparation time: 20–25 minutes
Cooking time: 1 hour 10 minutes

Each serving contains
Kcals: 330
g fat: 16
g saturated fat: 7.5

Bhuna gosht is a much loved dish in northern India. Its home is Delhi, the food-lover's paradise, where the exquisite Mogul cuisine dominates the scene. Bhuna, an important technique in Indian cooking, is similar to stir-frying. Spices are stir-fried in oil or ghee over a high heat, and a little water is added occasionally to ensure that they do not stick to the pan. In this version, I have fried the meat and the spices together in the fat naturally present in lamb and the result is delicious.

675g (1½lb) boneless shoulder of lamb,
cut into 2.5cm (1in) cubes, plus a few bones

55g (2oz) low-fat plain yogurt

2 large onions, finely sliced

1 tablespoon Ginger Purée (see page 16)

1 tablespoon Garlic Purée (see page 15)

10–12 black peppercorns

4 brown cardamom pods, slit slightly on top

6 cloves

2 x 5cm (2in) pieces of cinnamon stick, halved

2 bay leaves

1–3 dried red chillies, chopped

1 tablespoon Ground Roasted Cumin (see page 20)

2 teaspoons Ground Roasted Coriander (see page 21)

½ teaspoon ground turmeric

½–1 teaspoon chilli powder

1 teaspoon salt or to taste

1 tablespoon tomato purée

450ml (15fl oz) warm water

½ teaspoon Garam Masala (see page 22)

2 tablespoons chopped fresh coriander leaves

1–2 tomatoes, chopped

- Place the lamb in a non-stick saucepan with the bones. Add the yogurt, onions, ginger and garlic purées, peppercorns, cardamoms, cloves, cinnamon stick, bay leaves and dried red chillies. Place the pan over medium-high heat and stir until the contents begin to sizzle. Reduce the heat to medium, cover the pan and cook for 30 minutes.

- Remove the lid and increase the heat to high. Add the cumin, ground coriander, turmeric, chilli powder and salt. Cook, stirring constantly for 8–9 minutes. The spices will begin to stick to the pan halfway through – immediately add 2–3 tablespoons cold water and continue cooking, stirring, for 2–3 minutes. Repeat this process, adding cold water twice more.

- Stir in the tomato purée and warm water until thoroughly mixed and reduce the heat to low, then cover the pan and cook for 20 minutes.

- Remove the lid and cook for a few minutes to reduce the sauce, if necessary, until it is thick enough to coat the meat.

- Stir in the garam masala, coriander leaves and tomatoes. Cook for 1 minute, then remove and discard the bones. Serve with any bread or boiled basmati rice and a vegetable dish.

DRY-FRIED LAMB

Mangsher Jhalfrezi

Preparation time: 15–20 minutes
Cooking time: 55–60 minutes

SERVES 4

Each serving contains
Kcals: 316
g fat: 15.5
g saturated fat: 7.5

Jhalfrezi is one of the most popular dishes from the rich and varied cuisine of Bengal. In the Bengali language the word jhal *means hot, but a jhalfrezi is not meant to be chilli hot; instead the heat comes from freshly ground black pepper and other spices such as cloves, cinnamon and cardamom. The dish has a deliciously pungent thick sauce and is often garnished with fried onions, but for a lower-fat result you can add Browned Sliced Onions (page 18).*

675g (1½lb) boneless leg of lamb, cubed

1 large onion, finely chopped

1 tablespoon Ginger Purée (see page 16)

1 tablespoon Garlic Purée (see page 15)

1 teaspoon freshly ground black pepper

6 cloves

2.5cm (1in) piece of cinnamon stick

4 green cardamom pods, bruised

1 teaspoon paprika

½ teaspoon ground turmeric

2 teaspoons Ground Roasted Cumin (see page 20)

2 teaspoons Ground Roasted Coriander (see page 21)

75g (2½oz) low-fat plain yogurt

450ml (15fl oz) warm water

1½ tablespoons tomato purée

1 teaspoon salt or to taste

1–2 green chillies, seeded and sliced lengthways

2 tablespoons chopped fresh coriander leaves

- In a non-stick saucepan, about 30cm (12in) in diameter, dry-fry half the meat over high heat for 3–4 minutes. Add the remaining meat and continue to cook, stirring frequently, until the meat begins to release its juices.

- Add the onion and cook for 5 minutes, stirring frequently. Stir in the ginger and garlic purées, and continue to cook for 8–9 minutes or until all the liquid evaporates. Reduce the heat to medium halfway through cooking.

- Add the pepper, cloves, cinnamon stick, cardamoms, paprika, turmeric, cumin and ground coriander, and stir-fry for 1 minute, then add half the yogurt. Continue to stir-fry for a further 1 minute. Add the remaining yogurt and cook for 30–40 seconds.

- Pour in the water, then stir in the tomato purée and salt. Bring to the boil, cover and reduce the heat to low, then cook for 30–35 minutes or until the lamb is tender.

- Remove the lid and cook over medium heat for 3–4 minutes or until the sauce has thickened. Stir in the chillies and coriander leaves and cook for 1 minute. Serve with Chapatis (see page 159) and a raita.

---

* **VARIATION: You can use chicken instead of the lamb, but reduce the amount of water to 240ml (8fl oz). The cooking time is about 20 minutes for boneless chicken or 30–35 minutes for chicken on the bone.**

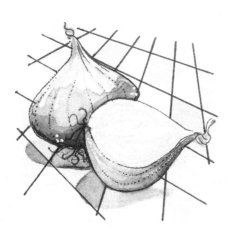

BAKED KEBABS

Dum ke Kabab

Preparation time: 10 minutes
Cooking time: 35 minutes

Each serving contains
Kcals: 425
g fat: 23.5
g saturated fat: 8.5

This recipe is based on a traditional north-Indian dish in which minced mutton is used. I have used lean minced lamb, although you could use minced chicken or turkey instead. It is excellent served with Fruit Raita (see page 179) and any bread.

10–12 blanched almonds, roughly chopped

2 tablespoons channa dhal or yellow split peas

1 tablespoon sunflower seeds

2–3 dried red chillies, chopped

2 tablespoons white poppy seeds

675g (1½lb) lean minced lamb

1 tablespoon Ginger Purée (see page 16)

1 tablespoon Garlic Purée (see page 15)

½ teaspoon ground turmeric

1 teaspoon paprika

1 tablespoon finely chopped fresh mint leaves or
½ teaspoon dried mint

2 tablespoons chopped fresh coriander leaves

1 teaspoon Garam Masala (see page 22)

1 teaspoon salt or to taste

Garnish

2 eggs, hard-boiled and sliced

1 red onion, halved and finely sliced

1 large tomato, sliced

wedges of lime or lemon

1 green chilli, seeded and cut into julienne strips

- Preheat a small frying pan over medium heat. When hot, turn the heat down to low and add the almonds. Stir for 1 minute, then add the channa dhal, sunflower seeds and chillies (in this order). Stir and roast for 1 minute, then add the poppy seeds. Roast for a further 1 minute, stirring, then remove from the heat. Do not allow the poppy seeds to darken. Transfer the ingredients to a plate. Allow to cool, then grind them in a coffee or spice mill until fine. Do not worry if the almonds are not finely ground.

- Put the lamb in a large bowl and add the ground mixture along with all the remaining ingredients. Mix thoroughly and knead for 1–2 minutes. Cover and set aside for 30 minutes. Meanwhile, preheat the oven to 190°C/ 375°F/Gas 5.

- Spread the spiced lamb in a 30 x 15cm (12 x 6in) ovenproof dish. Using the back of a metal spoon, tidy up the edges by pushing them inwards to make a neat, oblong shape, then smooth the top. Bake for 30 minutes.

- Allow to rest for 3–4 minutes, then cut into squares and transfer to a serving dish. Strain the cooking juices, brush a little over the kebabs and discard the remainder. Serve surrounded with the garnishing ingredients.

---

* **COOK'S TIP: Roasted channa dhal and white poppy seeds add a distinctive flavour. You can get these from Indian stores, large supermarkets and health food shops.**

MARINATED LEG OF LAMB

Raan

Each serving contains
Kcals: 490
g fat: 28
g saturated fat: 11.5

Preparation time: 30 minutes, plus marinating
Cooking time: 1 hour 40 minutes

The method of cooking a raan (leg of lamb) was first invented by the Mongolian warrior Chengiz Khan (AD 1162–1227), when it was known as the Chengezi Raan. The lamb was flavoured with a simple spice mix and roasted on a spit over a wood fire. Since then the recipe has been refined and different versions have been created, many elevated to such grand styles that they graced the tables of Emperors and Maharajas. My version has a fabulously opulent flavour despite being free from the usual ghee or butter.

3kg (6½lb) leg of lamb

75ml (2½fl oz) light malt vinegar

1½ teaspoons salt or to taste

225g (8oz) low-fat plain yogurt

1½ tablespoons Ginger Purée (see page 16)

1½ tablespoons Garlic Purée (see page 15)

75g (2½oz) Browned Onion Purée (see page 19)

pinch of saffron threads, pounded

½ teaspoon ground turmeric

1 teaspoon black peppercorns

seeds from 6 green cardamom pods

4 cloves

1 blade of mace

1½ tablespoons white poppy seeds

1 tablespoon sesame seeds

30g (1oz) unroasted cashew nut pieces

30g (1oz) raisins

150ml (5fl oz) boiling water

1 tablespoon flaked almonds, toasted, to garnish

- Trim excess fat and any membrane from the lamb. Prick it all over with the point of a small sharp knife or a fork. Place the lamb in a large shallow dish and pour the vinegar over it, then sprinkle with the salt. Rub the salt well into the meat, then set it aside.

- Mix the yogurt, ginger, garlic and onion purées, saffron and turmeric. Grind the peppercorns, cardamom seeds, cloves, mace, poppy and sesame seeds to a fine powder in a coffee or spice mill and stir into the yogurt mixture.

- Transfer the lamb to a large dish, discarding the vinegar, and rub the yogurt mixture all over the meat. Cover and chill for 24–36 hours. Bring the lamb to room temperature before cooking.

- Preheat the oven to 220°C/ 425°F/Gas 7. Put the leg of lamb in a roasting tin and cover with foil, tenting the foil so that it does not touch the meat. Alternatively, use a lidded roasting dish.

- Cook for 20 minutes, then reduce the temperature to 190°C/375°F/Gas 5. Cook for a further 35 minutes.

- Meanwhile, soak the cashews and raisins in the boiling water for 15 minutes, then purée them in a blender with the water in which they were soaked. Baste the meat generously with the cooking juices, then spread with the puréed nut mixture. Cover and continue cooking for 30–35 minutes.

- Uncover and baste the lamb, then cook for 8–10 minutes. Remove the meat from the oven, cover it loosely with foil and set it aside to rest for 15–20 minutes. To serve, cut the meat into chunky pieces and pour over any cooking juices left in the roasting dish. Garnish with the toasted almonds and serve. Spiced Chapatis (see page 160) or Vegetable Pilau (see page 158) and a raita are suitable accompaniments.

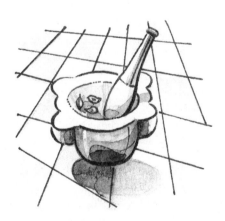

LAMB IN COCONUT MILK

SERVES 4

Nariyal ka Gosht

Preparation time: 20 minutes, plus marinating
Cooking time: 1 hour 10 minutes

Each serving contains
Kcals: 380
g fat: 24
g saturated fat: 15

This delectable dish originates from the southern coastal region where coconut palm is a major crop. Besides being used extensively in cooking, a thriving industry has developed around the non-food by-products of coconut.

The fat content of this recipe is quite high as it contains creamed coconut (the only recipe in the book to do so). Treat it as an occasional luxury.

75g (2½oz) low-fat plain yogurt

1 tablespoon Ginger Purée (see page 16)

1 tablespoon Garlic Purée (see page 15)

1 large onion, finely chopped

½ teaspoon ground turmeric

½–1 teaspoon chilli powder

1 teaspoon paprika

675g (1½lb) boneless leg of lamb,
cut into 2.5cm (1in) cubes, plus 225g (8oz) bones

1½ tablespoons Ground Roasted Coriander (see page 21)

1½ teaspoons Ground Roasted Cumin (see page 20)

55g (2oz) creamed coconut, grated, or desiccated coconut,
ground in a coffee or spice mill until smooth

300ml (10fl oz) warm water

1 teaspoon salt or to taste

½ teaspoon Garam Masala (see page 22)

2–3 green chillies, with the stalks intact

2–3 tablespoons chopped fresh coriander leaves

1 tablespoon lime juice

- Mix the yogurt, ginger and garlic purées, onion, turmeric, chilli powder and paprika in a large mixing bowl and add the meat. Mix thoroughly, cover the bowl and leave to marinate for 2 hours or overnight in the refrigerator. Bring it to room temperature before cooking.

- Put the marinated meat in a non-stick saucepan, about 30cm (12in) in diameter, and place over high heat. Stir until the meat begins to sizzle. Reduce the heat to low, cover the pan and cook for 25–30 minutes, stirring occasionally. There should be very little liquid left at the end of the cooking time (2–3 tablespoons). If necessary, cook, uncovered, over medium heat to reduce the liquid.

- Add the ground coriander and cumin, and cook over low heat for 3–4 minutes, stirring frequently. Stir in the coconut, warm water and salt. Cover the pan and simmer for 20–25 minutes, stirring occasionally.

- Add the garam masala, chillies and coriander leaves. Cook, uncovered, for 1–2 minutes, then stir in the lime juice and remove from the heat. Remove the bones and serve with Cinnamon Rice (see page 147) and Fresh Vegetable Pickle (see page 186).

---

* **COOK'S TIP: If you have any prepared Aromatic Stock (see page 23), use it instead of the water in the above recipe and omit the bones.**

LAMB WITH SPINACH

SERVES 4

Palak Gosht

Preparation time: 20–25 minutes
Cooking time: 1 hour 10 minutes

Each serving contains
Kcals: 325
g fat: 16
g saturated fat: 7.5

Lamb with spinach originated in Punjab, a state known for its rugged richness. The Punjabis are an energetic and fun-loving people with a particular flair for good food. Wheat and maize grow abundantly in the state (known as the granary of the nation) and Punjabis thrive on bread. Traditionally, this dish would be drenched in ghee, but this oil-free version has its own characteristic taste and aroma. Serve it with any bread in the true Punjabi style.

675g (1½lb) boneless shoulder or leg of lamb,
cut into 2.5cm (1in) cubes, plus a few bones

55g (2oz) low-fat plain yogurt

1 tablespoon Garlic Purée (see page 15)

1 tablespoon Ginger Purée (see page 16)

1 tablespoon ground coriander

1½ teaspoons ground cumin

2 x 5cm (2in) pieces of cinnamon stick, halved

6 green cardamom pods, bruised

½ teaspoon ground turmeric

½–1 teaspoon chilli powder

225g (8oz) Boiled Onion Purée (see page 17)

1 tablespoon tomato purée

1 teaspoon salt or to taste

300ml (10fl oz) warm water

225g (8oz) fresh spinach, finely chopped,
or frozen leaf spinach, thawed and drained

½ teaspoon Garam Masala (see page 22)

Garnish

1 tomato, finely chopped

1 tablespoon chopped fresh coriander leaves

● Put the meat into a non-stick saucepan and add the bones. Add the yogurt, garlic and ginger purées, ground coriander, cumin, cinnamon stick, cardamoms, turmeric and chilli powder. Place over medium-high heat and stir until the mixture begins to sizzle. Reduce the heat to low, cover and cook for 30–35 minutes, stirring occasionally. Remove the lid and increase the heat to high. Cook until all the liquid evaporates, stirring frequently.

- Add the boiled onion purée, tomato purée and salt. Continue to cook, stirring constantly, for a further 3–4 minutes. Pour in the warm water and bring to the boil. Reduce the heat to low, cover the pan and cook for 20–25 minutes or until the meat is tender.

- Add the spinach and stir until the leaves wilt. Cook, uncovered, over a medium heat for 3–4 minutes, stirring occasionally. Reduce the heat to low, cover the pan and cook for 5–7 minutes.

- Finally, stir in the garam masala and cook for 1 minute. Transfer to a serving dish and garnish with the chopped tomato. Sprinkle with chopped coriander and serve immediately.

Pork Main Meals

We tend to think of pork as a fatty meat and, therefore, not suitable for healthy eating. In fact, with the exception of some cuts and many pork products (such as sausages, belly of pork and streaky bacon) pork is one of the leanest meats available.

On reading about different types and cuts of meat to include in this book, I was surprised to discover that, not only is pork lower in fat than lamb or beef, but also it is only marginally fattier than chicken (with skin). Pork is a protein food which offers all the B vitamins, iron and zinc. As long as all the visible fat is removed, pork fits in extremely well as part of a healthy diet.

In Indian cooking, because of various religious taboos and socio-economic conditions, pork is not a widely used meat. Besides Goa, on the west coast, where an excellent range of pork dishes are cooked, only the tribal people in the hilly terrains of the north-east cook pork extensively.

SPICED MINCED PORK WITH MUSHROOMS

Kheema-Khumb Masala

Each serving contains
Kcals: 200
g fat: 8.5
g saturated fat: 2.9

Preparation time: 10 minutes, plus marinating
Cooking time: 22–25 minutes

This easy recipe makes a quick mid-week meal. It is a dry dish for which dhal or a vegetable curry are ideal accompaniments. Serve either Chapatis (see page 159) or boiled basmati rice to complete the meal

450g (1lb) lean minced pork

2 teaspoons Ginger Purée (see page 16)

2 teaspoons Garlic Purée (see page 15)

½ teaspoon ground turmeric

½ teaspoon chilli powder

55g (2oz) low-fat plain yogurt

1 teaspoon Ground Roasted Cumin (see page 20)

2 teaspoons Ground Roasted Coriander (see page 21)

225g (8oz) Boiled Onion Purée (see page 17)

1 teaspoon salt or to taste

225g (8oz) button mushrooms, quartered

1 tablespoon tomato purée

½ teaspoon Garam Masala (see page 22)

1–2 green chillies, seeded and cut into julienne strips

2 tablespoons finely chopped fresh coriander leaves

- In a mixing bowl, combine the minced pork, ginger and garlic purées, turmeric, chilli powder and yogurt. Mix thoroughly, cover and set aside for 30 minutes.

- Put the mixture in a non-stick sauté pan or frying pan, at least 25cm (10in) in diameter. Cook over medium-high heat for 7–8 minutes, stirring regularly, until the mixture is dry.

- Add the cumin and ground coriander. Continue to cook for 1 minute, then add the onion purée and salt, and cook for a further 3–4 minutes, stirring regularly.

- Mix in the mushrooms and tomato purée. Sprinkle 2–3 tablespoons water over the mixture and cover the pan. Reduce the heat to low and cook for 8–10 minutes, stirring once or twice to ensure that the contents do not stick to the bottom of the pan. If dry, add a little more water.

- Stir in the garam masala, chillies and fresh coriander leaves. Cook for 1 minute, then serve immediately.

GOAN PORK CURRY

SERVES 4

Pork Baffado

Preparation time: 15–20 minutes, plus marinating
Cooking time: 55–60 minutes

Each serving contains
Kcals: 308
g fat: 12
g saturated fat: 4.3

Goa is probably the only state in India where pork and beef are sold and consumed as a matter of habit. Hindus, who do not eat beef, and Muslims, who do not eat pork, live in close harmony with Christians, and each group respects the others' choice of meat. The cuisine of Goa has a predominantly Portuguese influence.

675g (1½lb) boneless leg of pork

2 tablespoons cider vinegar

2 teaspoons Ginger Purée (see page 16)

2 teaspoons Garlic Purée (see page 15)

½ teaspoon ground turmeric

2 teaspoons paprika

250ml (8½fl oz) medium-sweet cider

2.5cm (1in) piece of cinnamon stick, broken up

6 cloves

½ teaspoon black peppercorns

½ teaspoon black mustard seeds

1½ teaspoons cumin seeds

1 teaspoon salt or to taste

1 teaspoon soft brown sugar

250g (9oz) Boiled Onion Purée (see page 17)

1 tablespoon tomato purée

350ml (11fl oz) warm water

2–4 green chillies, seeded and cut into julienne strips

- Remove the rind and any visible fat from the pork. Cut the lean meat into 2.5cm (1in) cubes and put into a large mixing bowl.

- Mix the vinegar, ginger and garlic purées, turmeric and paprika, and pour over the meat. Stir until the meat is fully coated, then cover the bowl and set aside for 1–2 hours or overnight in the refrigerator. Bring it to room temperature before cooking.

- Put the marinated meat in a non-stick saucepan, about 30cm (12in) in diameter, and place over medium-high heat. Stir for 4–5 minutes or until the pork turns opaque.

- Pour in the cider and bring to simmering point. Cover the pan and reduce the heat to medium-low, then cook for 35–40 minutes or until the liquid

116 *Fat Free Indian Cookery*

resembles a thin batter.

- Meanwhile, preheat a small pan over medium heat. When hot, reduce the heat to low and add the whole spices. Roast the spices gently for 30–60 seconds, stirring all the time, until they release their aroma, then transfer them to a plate and cool for a few minutes.

- Grind the spices finely in a coffee or spice mill and add to the meat with the salt and sugar. Increase the heat slightly and cook until all the liquid has evaporated, stirring frequently.

- Add the onion purée and continue to cook for a further 3–4 minutes, then stir in the tomato purée and water. Reduce the heat to low, cover the pan and simmer gently for 8–10 minutes or until the sauce has thickened.

- Add the chillies and simmer for a further 1–2 minutes. Serve with boiled basmati rice or Cinnamon Rice (see page 147) and Cucumber and Peanut Salad (see page 188).

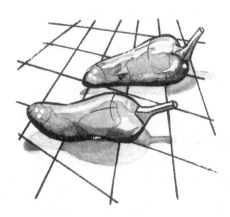

PORK VINDALOO

Shikar Vindaloo

Preparation time: 20 minutes, plus marinating
Cooking time: 55–60 minutes

Each serving contains
Kcals: 306
g fat: 12.5
g saturated fat: 4.4

Although vindaloo is probably the most famous export from Goa, its origins are Portuguese. Portuguese traders landed on the west coast of India in the sixteenth century in search of silks, spices and ivory, and history has it that they carried pork, preserved in vinegar, garlic and black pepper, to last their voyage. The word vin *comes from vinegar and* aloo *is derived from* alho, *meaning garlic in Portuguese. The recipe has been changed to a great extent by Indian influence and this is a low-fat version.*

675g (1½lb) boneless leg of pork

4 green cardamom pods

4 cloves

2.5cm (1in) piece of cinnamon stick, broken

½ teaspoon black mustard seeds

¼ teaspoon fenugreek seeds

½ teaspoon black peppercorns

3–8 dried red chillies, coarsely chopped

2 teaspoons Ginger Purée (see page 16)

2 teaspoons Garlic Purée (see page 15)

2 tablespoons cider vinegar

250ml (8½fl oz) medium-sweet cider

2 teaspoons paprika

1¼ teaspoons salt or to taste

250g (9oz) Boiled Onion Purée (see page 17)

350ml (11fl oz) warm water

½ teaspoon tamarind concentrate or 1 tablespoon tamarind pulp

1 teaspoon soft brown sugar

- Remove the rind from the pork and trim off any visible fat. Cut the lean meat into 2.5cm (1in) cubes and put in a large bowl.

- Preheat a small pan over medium heat. When hot, reduce the heat to low and add all the whole spices and dried red chillies. Roast the spices gently for 30–60 seconds, stirring all the time, until they release their aroma. Transfer the spices to a plate and leave to cool for 5 minutes, then grind them finely in a coffee or spice mill.

- Thoroughly mix the ginger and garlic purées, vinegar and the ground roasted spices, then add to the meat. Stir until the meat is fully coated, cover and leave to marinate for 2–3 hours or overnight in the refrigerator. Bring the meat to room temperature before cooking.

Put the meat and its marinade in a non-stick saucepan, about 30cm (12in) in diameter, and place over medium-high heat. Stir until the pork turns opaque, then pour in the cider. Bring just to the boil, cover the pan and cook over medium-low heat for 35–40 minutes or until the liquid is reduced to the consistency of a thin batter.

Uncover the pan and increase the heat slightly. Continue to cook for a further 3–4 minutes or until the moisture has evaporated completely.

Add the paprika and salt, cook for 2–3 minutes stirring constantly, then stir in the onion purée. Continue to cook for 4–5 minutes, stirring regularly.

Pour in the water and stir in the tamarind and sugar. Cover and simmer gently for 10–12 minutes, stirring occasionally. Serve with boiled basmati rice and a raita or a dry spiced vegetable dish.

VARIATION: Use leg of lamb instead of the pork.

SPICED PORK CHOPS

SERVES 4

Each serving contains
Kcals: 220
g fat: 10.5
g saturated fat: 4.7

Masala Chaamp

Preparation time: 15–20 minutes, plus marinating
Cooking time: 15 minutes

Marinated pork chops are delicious when pan roasted or grilled. As well as yogurt, I have used a little pineapple in the marinade as the enzyme it contains is an excellent tenderizing agent. Serve with Aubergine Pilau (see page 156) and Pineapple Raita (see page 178).

4 pork chops or boned shoulder or leg steaks

Marinade

85g (3oz) low-fat plain yogurt

85g (3oz) half-fat crème fraîche

85g (3oz) fresh pineapple, coarsely chopped

2–3 tablespoons chopped onions

2 teaspoons Ginger Purée (see page 16)

2 teaspoons Garlic Purée (see page 15)

½ teaspoon ground turmeric

½–1 teaspoon chilli powder

1 teaspoon salt or to taste

½ teaspoon sugar

Basting sauce

1 teaspoon Ground Roasted Cumin (see page 20)

¼ teaspoon chilli powder (optional)

1 teaspoon tomato ketchup

1 tablespoon finely chopped fresh coriander leaves

1 teaspoon sugar

pinch of salt

- Remove any rind and excess fat from the chops. Prick the chops all over with a fork to allow flavours to penetrate, then put them in a shallow dish.

- Put all the ingredients for the marinade in a blender or food processor and blend or process until well mixed. Pour this marinade over the chops and mix thoroughly. Cover and refrigerate for 4–6 hours or overnight. Bring the chops to room temperature before cooking.

- Preheat the grill to high for 8–10 minutes. Line the grill pan (without the rack) with aluminium foil. Lightly brush the foil with oil.

- Using a pair of tongs, lift each chop out of the dish and shake off any excess marinade back into the dish. Place the chops on the prepared grill pan and cook, 7.5cm (3in) away from the heat source, for 4–5 minutes or until the chops are slightly charred. Turn them over and cook for a further 3–4 minutes or until charred as before.

Mix all the ingredients for the basting sauce with the remaining marinade and add 2 tablespoons water, then brush half the mixture over the chops. Cook for 2–3 minutes, turn the chops over and repeat with the remaining basting sauce.

Transfer the chops to a warmed serving plate and strain any remaining cooking sauce over them. Serve immediately.

MEATBALL CURRY

Kofta Kari

Preparation time: 20–25 minutes
Cooking time: 40–45 minutes

Each serving contains
Kcals: 200
g fat: 8
g saturated fat: 2.8

Lean pork meatballs, simmered in a rich tomato sauce, are a delicious alternative to the traditional lamb or mutton version. Buy good-quality lean minced pork from supermarkets or make it yourself at home by removing all visible fat and chopping the meat into small pieces, then processing in the food processor until finely ground.

Meatballs

450g (1lb) lean minced pork

2 teaspoons Ginger Purée (see page 16)

1 teaspoon Garlic Purée (see page 15)

1–2 green chillies, seeded and chopped

1 small onion, coarsely chopped

15g (½oz) fresh coriander leaves and stalks

1 teaspoon salt or to taste

1 teaspoon Garam Masala (see page 22)

Tomato sauce

**400g (14oz) can chopped tomatoes
or 450g (1lb) fresh tomatoes, skinned and chopped**

1–2 green chillies, seeded and chopped

1 teaspoon Garlic Purée (see page 15)

1 teaspoon Ginger Purée (see page 16)

5cm (2in) piece of cinnamon stick, halved

6 cloves

1 teaspoon salt or to taste

1½ teaspoons sugar

½ teaspoon Ground Roasted Cumin (see page 20)

2 tablespoons chopped fresh coriander leaves

- Line a grill pan (without the rack) with aluminium foil and brush lightly with oil.

- Put all the ingredients for the meatballs in a food processor and blend until smooth. Divide into 16 golf-ball-sized portions and shape into neat rounds by rotating and pressing gently between your palms so that the mixture is quite compact. Place the meatballs in a single layer on the prepared pan.

- Preheat the grill to high. Grill the meatballs 7.5cm (3in) below the heat source for 4–5 minutes or until browned. Turn the meatballs and cook for 3–4 minutes or until browned. Remove and set aside.

- Put all the ingredients for the sauce (except the ground cumin and fresh coriander leaves) in a saucepan and add 75ml (2½fl oz) water. Bring to simmering point, cover and cook for 15 minutes.

- Cool the sauce slightly, remove the whole spices and either purée in a blender or press through a sieve.

- Put the cooked meatballs in a non-stick saucepan and pour the sauce over. Cover and cook over low heat for 12–15 minutes, stirring occasionally.

- Stir in the ground cumin and fresh coriander until thoroughly mixed. Serve with any bread or boiled basmati rice, and a raita or salad.

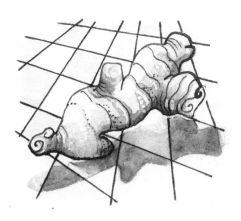

SPICED PORK BURGERS

SERVES 4

Masala Shikar ki Tikki

Each serving contains
Kcals: 200
g fat: 8.5
g saturated fat: 3

Preparation time: 10–15 minutes
Cooking time: 10–12 minutes

I had to include this recipe for my children, and all other children, who have a taste for spicy food. The meat is bound with bread soaked in milk. The lactic acid in the milk tenderizes the meat, giving a melt-in-the-mouth result. Lean minced lamb or chicken can be used instead of pork. I serve these with French fries made by coating the cut potatoes with a little olive oil and cooking them in a hot oven.

1 large slice of white bread, crusts removed

75ml (2½fl oz) semi-skimmed milk

450g (1lb) lean minced pork

1 teaspoon Ginger Purée (see page 16)

1 teaspoon Garlic Purée (see page 15)

30g (1oz) fresh coriander leaves and stalks

1 teaspoon Garam Masala (see page 22)

1 teaspoon salt or to taste

2 tablespoons finely chopped spring onions

Basting sauce

½ teaspoon ground cumin

1 tablespoon tomato ketchup

To serve

4 burger buns

4 slices of half-fat cheese (optional)

- Soak the bread in the milk for 5 minutes, then squeeze out the milk. Put the bread in a food processor with the remaining ingredients except the spring onions. Blend until smooth, then transfer the mixture to a bowl and add the spring onions. Mix well.

- Divide the mixture into quarters and shape each portion into a burger.

- Preheat the grill to high and blend the ingredients for the basting sauce together in a small bowl, adding 60ml (2fl oz) water.

- Cook the burgers 12cm (5in) below the heat source for 4–5 minutes. Brush with basting sauce and cook for a further 2–3 minutes. Turn the burgers and brush with the remaining sauce. Cook for 3–4 minutes.

- Meanwhile, split and warm the buns and spread them with more tomato ketchup, if liked. Place a burger on the bottom half of each bun and top with cheese (if using). Place under the grill until the cheese begins to melt. Place the tops of the buns on the burgers and serve immediately.

Vegetarian
Main Meals

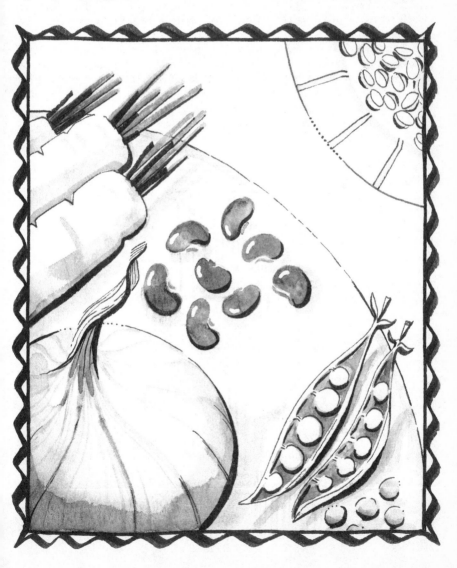

Although I am not a strict vegetarian, I have been brought up to believe that a vegetarian diet maintains a healthy mind as well as a healthy body. In recent years, the trend towards eating wholesome vegetarian food has gathered momentum, with an accusing finger pointed squarely at red meat, animal fat and sweets. Although the tendency towards eating vegetarian meals is now more common in the west, many people are still concerned about whether a solely vegetarian diet provides the essential nutrients required by the body.

In this section, I have grouped the dishes containing vegetarian protein. Pulses are the cheapest alternative to meat and combining them with vegetables and a staple, such as rice or bread, is the simple principle of a healthy and balanced vegetarian diet. As well as providing protein, they are also low in fat and high in fibre, and provide important vitamins and minerals.

India grows an amazing array of beans and lentils, which are used imaginatively to make a variety of dishes, from those for simple, everyday meals to elaborate and exotic creations. A lentil dish takes hardly any effort as most of the time is taken simmering the ingredients, during which time other dishes can be prepared for the meal.

There are literally thousands of different ways in which lentils are used in everyday Indian cooking. Whole lentils add a distinctive, nutty flavour to vegetable dishes. They can be soaked and ground, then mixed to a batter for making pancakes. Roasted and ground, they are used to make chutneys or to thicken sauces.

The other source of protein in the Indian vegetarian diet is paneer, the home-made Indian cheese, which is now produced on a commercial scale. In Britain, paneer is sold in all good supermarkets and, of course, in Indian stores. Cyprus halloumi cheese works extremely well as an alternative.

Please do not think that I am trying to convert you to a vegetarian diet – I am merely attempting to convince you to sample the simple joys of cooking and eating meals without fish, poultry or meat.

BUTTER BEANS WITH SPINACH

Pavta-Palak

Each serving contains
Kcals: 170
g fat: 7
g saturated fat: 3

Preparation time: 20 minutes
Cooking time: 35 minutes

Butter beans have a delicious nutty taste and a smooth, buttery texture. Dried beans have to be soaked for several hours and boiled until tender. Canned beans, if well rinsed, work very well and save time. Cooked with spinach, butter beans taste and look splendid.

1 tablespoon sunflower or soya oil

2.5cm (1in) piece of cinnamon stick

1 onion, finely chopped

1 teaspoon Ginger Purée (see page 16)

1–2 green chillies, seeded and finely chopped

½ teaspoon ground turmeric

½ teaspoon chilli powder

½ teaspoon Ground Roasted Cumin (see page 20)

1 teaspoon Ground Roasted Coriander (see page 21)

225g (8oz) tomatoes, skinned and chopped,
or canned chopped tomatoes with their juice

1 teaspoon salt or to taste

250g (9oz) spinach, finely chopped, or frozen leaf spinach

400g (14oz) can butter beans, drained and well rinsed

75ml (2½fl oz) single cream substitute

75ml (2½fl oz) warm water

- In a non-stick saucepan, heat the oil over low heat, then add the cinnamon stick and let it sizzle for 20–25 seconds. Add the onion, ginger purée and green chillies. Increase the heat slightly and fry for 5–6 minutes, stirring regularly to ensure even cooking.

- Stir in the turmeric, chilli powder, cumin and coriander. Cook for 30 seconds before adding the tomatoes. Continue to cook for 4–5 minutes, stirring frequently.

- Add the salt and spinach, and stir until the spinach wilts. Cover the pan and reduce the heat to low, then cook for 10 minutes.

- Add the butter beans, cream substitute and water. Re-cover and cook for a further 10 minutes. Serve with any bread or Cumin-Coriander Rice (see page 146).

CHICK PEAS IN TOMATO SAUCE

SERVES 4

Tamatar ka Rasewala Choley

Preparation time: 15 minutes
Cooking time: 30–35 minutes

Each serving contains
Kcals: 300
g fat: 11
g saturated fat: 1.3

Chick peas have a firm texture and satisfying, nutty flavour. They are delicious in this spicy tomato sauce, especially when served with fresh Indian bread and a refreshing raita.

2 tablespoons sunflower or soya oil

2 x 2.5cm (1in) pieces of cinnamon stick

6 green cardamom pods, bruised

6 cloves

1 large onion, finely chopped

1–2 green chillies, seeded and chopped

2 teaspoons Ginger Purée (see page 16)

½ teaspoon ground turmeric

¼–½ teaspoon chilli powder

225g (8oz) can chopped tomatoes, with their juice

2 x 400g (14oz) cans chick peas, drained and well rinsed

1¼ teaspoons salt or to taste

300ml (10fl oz) warm water

1 teaspoon Ground Roasted Cumin (see page 20)

1 tablespoon chopped fresh coriander leaves

1 tablespoon chopped fresh mint or ½ teaspoon dried mint

- Heat the oil in a non-stick saucepan, about 18cm (7in) in diameter, over low heat and add the cinnamon, cardamom and cloves. Let the spices sizzle gently for 20–25 seconds.

- Add the onion, chillies and ginger purée. Increase the heat slightly and cook, stirring regularly, for 8–10 minutes or until the onion begins to brown.

- Stir in the turmeric, chilli powder and tomatoes. Cook for a further 4–5 minutes, stirring frequently.

- Add the chick peas, salt and water. Bring to the boil, reduce the heat to low and cover the pan, then simmer for 12–15 minutes.

- Stir in the cumin, chopped coriander and mint. Simmer for 1–2 minutes, then serve with any bread and a raita.

---

* **VARIATION: Use black-eyed beans instead of the chick peas.**

CHICK PEAS WITH INDIAN CHEESE

Choley-Paneer

Preparation time: 20 minutes
Cooking time: 25 minutes

Each serving contains
Kcals: 244
g fat: 9.7
g saturated fat: 1.6

Paneer is used all over India in both sweet and savoury dishes. In this dish, halloumi cheese (from Cyprus) can be used instead, but reduce the quantity of salt by half, as halloumi is salted.

225g (8oz) paneer, cut into 5cm (2in) cubes

2 tablespoons sunflower or soya oil

1 small onion, finely chopped

2 teaspoons Ginger Purée (see page 16)

2 teaspoons Garlic Purée (see page 15)

1–2 green chillies, seeded and chopped

1¼ teaspoons salt or to taste

½ teaspoon ground turmeric

1 teaspoon Ground Roasted Cumin (see page 20)

¼–½ teaspoon chilli powder

125g (4½oz) Boiled Onion Purée (see page 17)

225g (8oz) tomatoes, skinned and chopped,
or canned chopped tomatoes with their juice

400g (14oz) can chick peas, drained and well rinsed

125g (4½oz) spinach, coarsely chopped, or frozen leaf spinach

- Bring a saucepan of water to the boil and add the paneer. Bring back to the boil and boil for 1 minute, then drain and set aside. This prepares the paneer to absorb all the flavours.

- Heat the oil over medium heat in a sauté pan, about 30cm (12in) in diameter, and add the onion, ginger and garlic purées, and green chilli. Fry for 2–3 minutes, then add the salt. The salt helps to draw out the onion juices, so that they cook longer without burning. Reduce the heat slightly and continue to cook for 5–7 minutes or until the onions are soft.

- Add the turmeric, cumin and chilli powder. Cook for 1 minute, then add the onion purée. Cook for a further 2–3 minutes.

- Increase the heat to medium and add the tomatoes. Cook for 2 minutes, then add the chick peas. Cook for 4–5 minutes, stirring regularly.

- Finally, add the paneer and spinach, and cook for 5–6 minutes, stirring. Serve with Puffed Grilled Bread (see page 161), Chapatis (see page 159) or Cinnamon Rice (see page 147) and a raita.

STEAMED SEMOLINA CAKES WITH SPICY LENTILS

SERVES 4–5,
MAKES 18 IDLIS

Idli-Sambar

Preparation time: 20 minutes, plus standing time
Cooking time: 45–50 minutes

Each serving contains
Kcals: 261
g fat: 4.9
g saturated fat: 0.8

Hot, soft and fluffy steamed cakes (idlis) served with spiced lentils is the signature dish of Tamil Nadu in southern India. Steamed cakes can be made with a combination of rice and lentils, which are soaked and ground, then left to ferment before steaming, but this recipe uses semolina, which is easier and quicker. Idli-Sambar makes a balanced vegetarian meal.

Idlis

280g (10oz) semolina

1 teaspoon baking powder

½ teaspoon bicarbonate of soda

½ teaspoon crushed dried chillies

15g (½oz) unroasted cashew nuts, chopped

1 tablespoon finely chopped fresh coriander leaves

½ teaspoon salt or to taste

225g (8oz) low-fat plain yogurt

450ml (15fl oz) soda water

Sambar

225g (8oz) toor dhal (see page 9)

½ teaspoon ground turmeric

1 carrot, cut into bite-sized dice

125g (4½oz) green beans, fresh or frozen, cut into 2.5cm (1in) pieces

1½ teaspoons salt or to taste

1 tablespoon coriander seeds

1 teaspoon cumin seeds

1–4 dried red chillies, broken up

½ teaspoon black peppercorns

½ teaspoon black mustard seeds

2 tablespoons tamarind juice or ½ teaspoon tamarind concentrate

2 tablespoons finely chopped fresh coriander leaves and stalks

- Prepare the mixture for the idlis. In a mixing bowl, mix all the dry ingredients. Beat the yogurt until smooth, then stir it into the semolina mixture.

- Gradually add the soda water and mix until you have a thick paste, slightly softer than the consistency of a dropping cake mixture. If the mixture has any lumps, whisk it with a wire whisk. Cover the bowl and set aside for 30 minutes.

- Meanwhile, put the dhal in a saucepan and add the turmeric. Pour in 1.2 litres (2 pints) water. Bring to the boil, then reduce the heat to medium and cook for 3–4 minutes or until all the foam subsides. Reduce the heat to low, cover the pan and cook for 20 minutes.

- Add the carrot, green beans and salt to the dhal, re-cover and continue to cook for a further 10–15 minutes or until the vegetables are tender.

- Lightly brush the cups from an egg poacher with oil and prepare a steamer over a saucepan of boiling water for cooking the idlis. Place 1½ tablespoons idli mixture into each cup and steam them for 10 minutes. When cooked, remove and keep hot until all the mixture is cooked.

- While the idlis are steaming, preheat a small pan over medium heat. Add the coriander seeds and cumin seeds, dried red chillies, peppercorns and mustard seeds, and reduce the heat to low. Stir and roast the spices for 30–60 seconds or until they begin to release their aroma. Transfer the spices to a plate and cool slightly, then grind to a fine powder in a coffee or spice mill.

- Add the ground roasted spices to the lentils followed by the tamarind. If you are using tamarind concentrate, stir until it is dissolved completely. Add the fresh coriander leaves, remove from the heat and serve with the steamed cakes.

---

* **NUTRITIONAL ANALYSIS NOTE Each idli provides 18Kcals; 0.8g fat (0.14g saturated fat). When served to 4, each portion of sambar provides 180 Kcals; 1.3g fat (0.16g saturated fat).**

---

* **COOK'S TIP: Traditionally, steel idli moulds are used to cook the cakes, and Indian housewives cook them in a pressure cooker. The cups from an egg poacher work just as well and a steamer will do the job instead of a pressure cooker. You can serve the idlis as a snack with a chutney, such as Almond Chutney (see page 183), instead of the sambar. The sambar can be served with boiled rice instead of the idlis.**

LENTILS WITH KIDNEY BEANS

Dhal Maharani

Preparation time: 10 minutes
Cooking time: 50 minutes

SERVES 4–6

Each serving contains
Kcals: 364
g fat: 13
g saturated fat: 5

A classic dish from the state of Punjab, where whole urad dhal (black grams) are cooked with kidney beans. I find channa dhal or yellow split peas more visually appealing than urad dhal, as well as being easily accessible.

170g (6oz) channa dhal (yellow split peas)

1 tablespoon grated fresh root ginger

2 green chillies, seeded and chopped

425g (15oz) can red kidney beans, drained and well rinsed

1 teaspoon salt or to taste

120ml (4fl oz) single cream substitute

2 tablespoons sunflower or vegetable oil

1 small onion, finely chopped

½ teaspoon ground turmeric

1 teaspoon Garam Masala (see page 22)

125g (4½oz) ripe tomatoes, chopped

2 tablespoons chopped fresh coriander leaves

- Wash the dhal or split peas thoroughly and put them in a heavy saucepan with half the ginger and half the chillies. Pour in 750ml (1¼ pints) water. Bring to the boil, then reduce the heat to low and simmer, uncovered, for 30 minutes or until tender. Mash some of the cooked dhal with a wooden spoon, pressing it against the side of the pan and mixing well to achieve a thick texture.

- Add the kidney beans, salt and cream substitute. Simmer for 10 minutes.

- Meanwhile, in a small saucepan, heat the oil over medium heat and fry the onion and remaining ginger and chillies for 6–7 minutes or until the onion is lightly browned.

- Stir in the turmeric and garam masala and cook for 1 minute, then add the tomatoes and coriander. Cook for a further 1 minute. Reserve 1 tablespoon of this mixture and stir the remainder into the peas and beans. Garnish with the reserved onion and tomato mixture and serve with any bread or rice.

SPICED MIXED LENTILS

Mila hua Masala Dhal

Preparation time: 15 minutes
Cooking time: 35 minutes

SERVES 5

Each serving contains
Kcals: 219
g fat: 6.3
g saturated fat: 0.8

As a rule, no Indian meal is complete without a lentil dish – to the vast majority of vegetarians it is a very satisfying and wholesome main dish, and meat-eaters enjoy lentils as a side dish. Here, I have combined three types of lentils, but you can vary the combination or cook just one of them.

75g (2½oz) red lentils

75g (2½oz) green lentils

75g (2½oz) skinless split mung beans (moong dhal)

2 tablespoons sunflower or soya oil

½ teaspoon black mustard seeds

½ teaspoon cumin seeds

2.5cm (1in) cube of fresh root ginger, cut into julienne strips

1–2 green chillies, seeded and cut into julienne strips

1–2 red chillies, seeded and cut into julienne strips

1 teaspoon ground turmeric

900ml (1½ pints) hot water

1 teaspoon salt or to taste

1 teaspoon Ground Roasted Cumin (see page 20)

2 tablespoons finely chopped fresh coriander leaves

- Wash the three types of lentils together and leave to drain in a colander.

- Heat the oil over low heat in a non-stick saucepan, about 18cm (7in) in diameter. When hot, add the mustard seeds. As soon as they pop, add the cumin seeds, followed by the ginger.

- Reserve a little of both types of chillies and add the remainder to the pan, then fry gently for 1–2 minutes.

- Add the turmeric and the lentils. Increase the heat slightly and fry for 4–5 minutes, stirring regularly, then pour in the water. Bring to the boil, reduce the heat to low, cover the pan and simmer for 25–30 minutes.

- Stir in the salt and cumin, and simmer for 1 minute.

- Stir in the fresh coriander leaves and remove from the heat. Serve garnished with the reserved chillies. Offer Tandoori Bread (see page 162) and a raita as accompaniments; Cumin-Coriander Rice (see page 146), a raita or a vegetable dish are also excellent with the lentils.

PANCAKES WITH
SPICY POTATO FILLING

Masala Dosa

Preparation time: 10–15 minutes
Cooking time: 30–35 minutes

Each serving contains
Kcals: 75
g fat: 2.6
g saturated fat: 1.2

Tamil Nadu in Southern India is the home of dosas, which are crispy pancakes filled with spiced potatoes and served with a chutney. The pancakes are traditionally made by grinding a mixture of rice and lentils together, then the mixture is fermented for 6–12 hours before cooking. This is my instant version, which is quite delicious.

Pancakes

125g (4½oz) semolina

125g (4½oz) ground rice

75g (2½oz) plain flour

½ teaspoon salt or to taste

150g (5½oz) low-fat plain yogurt

Filling

1 tablespoon desiccated coconut

2–4 dried red chillies, broken up

1 teaspoon Ground Roasted Cumin (see page 20)

1 teaspoon Ground Roasted Coriander (see page 21)

1 teaspoon salt or to taste

2 teaspoons lemon juice

1 tablespoon sunflower or soya oil

½ teaspoon black mustard seeds

½ teaspoon ground turmeric

550g (1¼lb) new potatoes, boiled and cut into bite-sized pieces

2 tablespoons chopped fresh coriander leaves

- First prepare the filling. Grind the coconut and chillies to a powder in a coffee or spice mill. Transfer the mixture to a small bowl and add the cumin, ground coriander, salt, lemon juice and 60ml (2fl oz) water. Mix and set aside.

- Heat the oil in a non-stick saucepan over low heat. Add the mustard seeds, then as soon as they start crackling, stir in the turmeric.

- Add the potatoes and the coconut mixture. Stir until the potatoes are heated through and the liquid is completely absorbed. Stir in the chopped coriander leaves, then keep the filling hot over very low heat while you make the pancakes.

- In a large mixing bowl mix the semolina, ground rice, flour and salt. Mix the yogurt with 375ml (13½fl oz) water, then gradually add to the semolina mixture, whisking well with a wire whisk. Alternatively, put all the ingredients in a blender or food processor and blend until smooth.

- Heat a large, heavy griddle or non-stick frying pan, at least 23cm (9in) in diameter, over medium heat and brush the surface lightly with oil. Wait until the surface of the pan is really hot, then pour about 125ml (4½fl oz) batter from a measuring jug, spreading it quickly and evenly on the pan. Allow the mixture to cook and set for 2 minutes.

- Sprinkle 1 tablespoon water around the edges, wait for 15–20 seconds, then turn the dosa over with a thin spatula or a fish slice. Cook for a further 2–3 minutes or until brown patches show through underneath.

- Place a little of the spiced potato mixture on top and roll it up. Keep hot until the remainder of the batter is cooked. Serve immediately, with Almond Chutney (see page 183).

---

* **COOK'S TIP: To keep the filled dosas hot, place them in a single layer in an ovenproof dish, cover with foil and place in a warm oven or hot grill compartment (with the heat source turned off). The filling and chutney can be made in advance and kept chilled until required. Reheat the filling gently in a non-stick pan or in the microwave.**

VEGETABLE KORMA

Subzi Korma

Preparation time: 30 minutes, plus soaking
Cooking time: 15 minutes

SERVES 4

Each serving contains
Kcals: 251
g fat: 13.4
g saturated fat: 2.5

Originating from royal kitchens, korma is a dish associated with affluence. Traditionally meat-based, various vegetarian kormas are made these days. This healthy eating version is based on the principles of a traditional northern korma, but, instead of using cream and/or full-fat dried milk, I have enriched the sauce with semi-skimmed milk and puréed cashew nuts. Sunflower seeds are also used to make up for the minimal use of cashews.

300ml (10fl oz) skimmed or semi-skimmed milk

30g (1oz) unroasted cashew nut pieces

15g (½oz) sunflower seeds

225g (8oz) carrots, cut diagonally into 3mm (⅛in) slices

125g (4½oz) baby corn cobs

2 teaspoons lemon juice

125g (4½oz) green beans, cut into 5cm (2in) pieces

340g (12oz) cauliflower, divided into 2.5cm (1in) florets

2 tablespoons sunflower or soya oil

½ teaspoon royal cumin or caraway seeds

2.5cm (1in) piece of cinnamon stick

4 green cardamom pods, bruised

1 small onion, finely chopped

1 teaspoon Ginger Purée (see page 16)

1 teaspoon Garlic Purée (see page 15)

1 tablespoon Ground Roasted Coriander (see page 21)

½ teaspoon chilli powder

225g (8oz) Boiled Onion Purée (see page 17)

1 teaspoon salt or to taste

- Bring half the milk to the boil, remove from the heat and add the cashews and sunflower seeds. Leave to soak for 15–20 minutes, then purée until smooth in a blender.

- Put the carrots and corn in a saucepan and add 450ml (15fl oz) water. Bring to the boil, then reduce the heat to medium and cook, uncovered, for 5 minutes.

- Add the lemon juice and beans, then pile the cauliflower on top. Cover the pan and cook for a further 5 minutes. Stir to reposition the vegetables halfway through.

- Spread out the vegetables, along with their cooking liquid, in a large dish or roasting tin. This will prevent the vegetables from overcooking.

- Heat the oil over low heat in a non-stick saucepan, about 30cm (12in) in diameter, and add the royal cumin seeds or caraway seeds, cinnamon stick and cardamom pods. Allow the spices to sizzle gently for 20–25 seconds, then add the onion, and ginger and garlic purées. Increase the heat slightly and fry the ingredients for 5–6 minutes or until the onions are soft.

- Add the ground coriander and chilli powder, cook for 30 seconds, then stir in the onion purée and cook for 3–4 minutes.

- Stir in the salt, the vegetables with all their cooking liquid, the blended cashew mixture and the remaining milk. Bring to simmering point, then cook for 5 minutes, stirring once or twice. Serve with Saffron Rice (see page 148) and Beetroot Raita (see page 181).

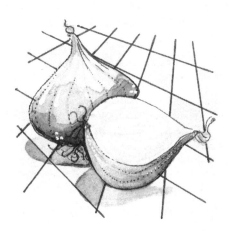

MUNG BEAN AND WATERMELON CURRY

SERVES 4

Sabut Moong aur Tarbooz ki Kari

Preparation time: 15 minutes, plus soaking
Cooking time: 20 minutes

Each serving contains
Kcals: 242
g fat: 6.4
g saturated fat: 0.9

Although mung beans need soaking for a few hours, they cook very quickly. Teamed with watermelon, they look striking and taste splendid. The watermelon releases its sweet juices into the beans which are tossed in ginger, chillies and cumin; a squeeze of lemon enhances the flavours.

225g (8oz) mung beans,
washed and soaked for 6–8 hours or overnight

¼ large watermelon, peeled and seeded

2 tablespoons sunflower or soya oil

½ teaspoon black mustard seeds

1 teaspoon grated fresh root ginger

1–2 green chillies, seeded and finely chopped

½–1 teaspoon chilli powder

½ teaspoon ground turmeric

1 teaspoon Ground Roasted Cumin (see page 20)

1¼ teaspoons salt or to taste

1 teaspoon sugar

150ml (5fl oz) warm water

2 tablespoons lemon juice

- Drain the beans and put into a saucepan with 450ml (15fl oz) water. Bring to the boil and skim off the froth from the surface. Reduce the heat to medium and cook for 12–15 minutes or until the beans are tender. Stir to ensure that the beans cook evenly. Reduce the heat to low for the last 5 minutes. The beans should remain whole and the water should be reduced to about 2–3 tablespoons. Remove from the heat and set aside.

- Cut the melon into 2.5cm (1in) cubes, making sure you collect all the juices in a bowl as you do so.

- Heat the oil over low heat in a saucepan. Add the mustard seeds and when they crackle, add the ginger and green chillies. Cook for 1 minute. Add the chilli powder, turmeric and half the cumin. Cook for 30 seconds.

- Add the beans, watermelon, salt and sugar. Increase the heat slightly and pour in the warm water. Cover and simmer for 4–5 minutes. Stir in the lemon juice and reserved cumin and remove from the heat.

- Serve with boiled basmati rice and Dry-spiced Okra (see page 168).

SPICED LENTILS

Masala Dhal

Each serving contains
Kcals: 240
g fat: 6.5
g saturated fat: 0.8

Red and green lentils are readily available and used in combination they look quite stunning. For a vegetarian menu, serve either Chapatis (see page 159) or rice and a vegetable dish as accompaniments. These lentils are also delicious with grilled fish, poultry or meat.

115g (4oz) red lentils

115g (4oz) green lentils

2 tablespoons sunflower or soya oil

2.5cm (1in) piece of cinnamon stick, halved

1 small onion, finely chopped

2 teaspoons Ginger Purée (see page 16)

2 teaspoons Garlic Purée (see page 15)

½–1 teaspoon chilli powder

½ teaspoon ground turmeric

1 teaspoon salt or to taste

115g (4oz) fresh tomatoes, skinned and chopped,
or canned chopped tomatoes, drained

900ml (1½ pints) warm water

2 tablespoons chopped fresh coriander leaves

Garnish

1 red chilli, seeded and cut into julienne strips

1 green chilli, seeded and cut into julienne strips

- Thoroughly wash both types of lentils together, then leave to drain in a colander.

- Heat the oil over medium heat in a non-stick saucepan. Add the cinnamon stick, onion and ginger and garlic purées. Fry for 4–5 minutes, stirring frequently, until the onion begins to brown.

- Stir in the lentils, chilli powder, turmeric and salt. Fry for 3–4 minutes, stirring frequently, then add the tomatoes. Cook for a further 2–3 minutes, stirring frequently.

- Pour in the water and bring to the boil. Reduce the heat to low, cover the pan and cook for 25–30 minutes.

- Stir in the fresh coriander leaves and cook, uncovered, for 1–2 minutes. Serve garnished with the red and green chillies.

SPICED OMELETTE CURRY

Masala Umlet ki Kari

Preparation time: 20 minutes
Cooking time: 15–20 minutes

Each serving contains
Kcals: 135
g fat: 10.3
g saturated fat: 2.3

This is a low-fat version of a speciality among the Muslim community in the southern coastal region of India. The omelettes are cut into strips, then tossed in a lightly spiced tomato sauce. This dish is delicious with Puffed Grilled Bread (see page 161) or Chapatis (see page 159). A salad or a dry-spiced vegetable dish will complete the meal.

Omelettes

4 large eggs

2 tablespoons finely chopped red onion

1 green chilli, seeded and finely chopped

½ teaspoon Ginger Purée (see page 16)

1 tablespoon finely chopped fresh coriander leaves

¼ teaspoon ground turmeric

½ teaspoon salt

a little sunflower or soya oil for brushing pan

Sauce

1 tablespoon sunflower or soya oil

½ teaspoon ground turmeric

½ teaspoon chilli powder

½ teaspoon salt or to taste

½ teaspoon sugar

225g (8oz) tomatoes, skinned and finely chopped

150ml (5fl oz) warm water

1 teaspoon Ground Roasted Cumin (see page 20)

1 tablespoon finely chopped fresh coriander leaves

- Make two omelettes. Whisk the eggs with 2 tablespoons water until frothy (the water makes the omelettes light and fluffy). Add the remaining ingredients and mix thoroughly.

- Brush a non-stick omelette pan, 12–15cm (5–6in) in diameter, with sunflower or soya oil and place over medium heat. Pour half the egg mixture into the hot pan and stir the middle of the mixture gently, rotating it for even cooking.

- Stop stirring and allow the egg to set, then turn the omelette over with a wide spatula. Cook the second side for 1–2 minutes. The omelette should resemble a thick pancake. Slide it out on to a board and cook the second omelette the same way.

- Cut the omelettes into strips, about 2.5cm (1in) wide, and cut the strips into 5cm (2in) lengths. Set aside.

- For the sauce, heat the oil over medium heat in a non-stick sauté pan. Add the turmeric, chilli powder, salt and sugar. Stir once, then add the tomatoes and cook for 3–4 minutes. Pour in the water, reduce the heat slightly and cook for a further 3–4 minutes, stirring frequently.

- Mix in the cumin and fresh coriander, then add the omelette strips. Reduce the heat to low and cook for 2–3 minutes. Stir gently once or twice, then serve immediately.

LENTILS WITH HOT OIL SEASONING

Tadka Dhal

Preparation time: 10 minutes
Cooking time: 30 minutes

Each serving contains
Kcals: 200
g fat: 3.5
g saturated fat: 0.5

Tadka (or tarka) is a very popular and quick cooking technique used to add instant flavour to dishes. A selection of dried whole spices are usually used, with one or more fresh flavouring ingredients added. The choice of spices is regional – the following is typical of east and north-east India.

225g (8oz) red lentils

1 teaspoon ground turmeric

1 teaspoon salt or to taste

1 tablespoon sunflower or soya oil

¼ teaspoon black mustard seeds

¼ teaspoon fennel seeds

¼ teaspoon cumin seeds

¼ teaspoon onion seeds

6–8 fenugreek seeds

1–4 dried red chillies

2 bay leaves, crumpled

2 tablespoons finely chopped fresh coriander leaves

- Wash and drain the lentils, then place in a saucepan. Pour in 900ml (1½ pints) water and add the turmeric. Bring to the boil, then reduce the heat to medium and cook, uncovered, for 5–6 minutes or until the foam subsides.

- Cover the pan and reduce the heat to low. Simmer for 20–25 minutes, then stir in the salt.

- In a small saucepan or a ladle, carefully heat the oil over medium heat. When hot, add the remaining ingredients, except the fresh coriander leaves, and switch off the heat. Allow the spices to sizzle in the hot oil for 20–25 seconds, then pour this mixture over the cooked lentils.

- Stir in the fresh coriander leaves and keep the pan covered until you are ready to serve the meal.

---

* **HEALTHY HINT: Lentils are ideal for a low-fat diet. They are high in fibre and protein.**

Rice &
Bread

In India, rice is considered to be the most valuable gift of nature and nearly half the population eats rice every day. Long-grain rice is the perfect partner for Indian dishes and basmati is the universally popular choice. While boiled rice and curry is the daily diet, pilaus and biryanis are cooked on special occasions.

Millions of years ago, early types of rice grew wild in parts of what is now South-East Asia, especially in water-logged fields. It was a form of grass, with miniature ears of grain at the top. Decades of cultivation and the use of natural organic fertilizers transformed the wild grass into the modern-day grain. Rice was first grown in northern Thailand and north-east India. Today, it is grown all over India and, because of the country's diverse geographical and climatic conditions, each region grows its own variety. The pride and joy of northern India is the exquisite basmati rice, which is the finest in the world. Southern India has its own variety of rice, known as *ambey mohur*, which has a subtle hint of mango fragrance (*ambey* meaning mango and *mohur* fragrance).

Bread is another important daily food. Wheat and barley have been the staple grains in northern India since ancient times. Like rice, through natural evolution grains of wild grasses have been transformed into what we know as wheat. Everyday breads, and most other types of flat breads, are unleavened and made from wholewheat flour. Leavened breads, such as the different types of naan, were introduced to India by Middle-Eastern invaders.

Most flat breads are cooked on a cast-iron griddle known as a *tava*; a standard griddle or a heavy frying pan can be used, but it is easier to handle the bread if you use a pan without raised sides. In an Indian home, bread is freshly made for each meal and that is the way to enjoy it at its best. The dough can be stored in a polythene bag in the refrigerator for 2–3 days, then brought to room temperature for 30 minutes before rolling and cooking.

When making dough, add the water gradually as it is difficult to be precise about the quantity required. Some flours are more absorbent than others, so you may have to adjust the quantity of water suggested in the recipe. Use a little dry flour to dust each piece of dough before rolling out.

Do not be tempted to reheat Indian bread in the microwave. This ancient food is not at all compatible with the our modern miracle worker! The best method is to wrap the bread in aluminium foil and place in a preheated oven at 325°F/160°C/Gas 3 for 6–8 minutes. Overheating makes the bread brittle. Cooked bread can be frozen; thaw and reheat as for cooled bread.

PERFECT COOKED RICE

Generally, you can cook rice by two simple methods. One is to boil the rice in plenty of water with a pinch of salt until the grains are tender, then drain it. This is fine for most long-grain rice, but basmati deserves a little special care to preserve its unique aroma and flavour. I prefer to cook basmati rice using the absorption method. Use the following simple rules and you will never be disappointed – they have never let me down!

- Weigh the quantity required accurately and wash the rice in cold water several times. The water will be cloudy for the first 2–3 changes of water, because of the starch in the rice. Wash the rice until the water runs clear, gently lifting and turning the grains, but do not rub them too hard.

- When the water is clear, soak the rice for 30 minutes, then drain it thoroughly in a colander.

- Use a saucepan that has a heavy base and is not too small (basmati rice expands considerably during cooking). As a guide, the saucepan should be about two-thirds full when the rice is cooked.

- Measure the water accurately. Once the lid goes on the saucepan, set the timer and do not worry about the rice until the time is up. Do not be tempted to lift the lid – it is important to keep the steam in the pan.

- The heat level is important for the final cooking time: turn it down to simmering point and use a heat diffuser, if necessary, for gentle cooking. I have never found it necessary to cook basmati rice for longer than 10 minutes, except when it is cooked with meat, seafood, vegetables or other ingredients.

- When the rice is cooked, remove the pan from the heat and let it rest for 8–10 minutes. Again, do not be tempted to uncover the pan. This is important because freshly cooked basmati rice is very fragile. Once it has had time to absorb the starch back into the grains, simply fluff up the rice with a fork and use a metal spoon to serve it.

---

* **HEALTHY HINT: Rice is an excellent food for babies and convalescents as it is nourishing and easily digested. Rice is also believed to cool the body. This is probably the reason why rice is the staple food in the sultry southern Indian climate whereas bread is more popular in the cooler north. Rice is a good source of carbohydrate which is an essential part of a healthy diet.**

CUMIN-CORIANDER RICE

Jeera-Dhania Chawal

**Preparation time: 5 minutes, plus soaking
Cooking time: 12–13 minutes**

Each serving contains
Kcals: 277
g fat: 3.5
g saturated fat: 0.3

When you have company, you may feel like cooking something special rather than boiled rice (although, to me, there is nothing to beat the aroma of freshly cooked plain basmati). This recipe is a simple one with a fairly neutral background and the ideal complement for any curry or spicy grilled meat or poultry.

225g (8oz) basmati rice, washed and soaked in cold water for 30 minutes

1 tablespoon sunflower or soya oil

1 teaspoon cumin seeds

1 teaspoon coriander seeds, crushed

¼ teaspoon ground turmeric

1 teaspoon salt or to taste

475ml (16fl oz) warm water

fresh coriander sprigs, to garnish

- Drain the rice and leave it to drain in a colander.

- Heat the oil in a non-stick saucepan over medium heat. Add the cumin seeds and coriander seeds and let them sizzle for 10–15 seconds.

- Add the rice, turmeric and salt. Fry the rice, stirring constantly, for 2 minutes, then pour in the warm water. Bring to the boil, reduce the heat to low and cover the pan tightly.

- Cook, undisturbed, for 10 minutes. Remove from the heat and allow to rest for 8–10 minutes, then fluff up the rice with a fork. Serve garnished with fresh coriander.

CINNAMON RICE

Dalchini Chawal

Preparation time: 2–3 minutes, plus soaking
Cooking time: 10–12 minutes

SERVES 4

Each serving contains
Kcals: 227
g fat: 3.5
g saturated fat: 0.3

This is a simple recipe for boiled rice flavoured with cinnamon and bay leaf. The Indian bay leaf comes from the cinnamon tree and it has a similar flavour to cinnamon. I have fond memories of plucking fresh cinnamon leaves for my mother and removing pieces of the bark to eat as a breath freshener!

225g (8oz) basmati rice, washed and soaked in cold water for 30 minutes

1 teaspoon sunflower or soya oil

½ teaspoon salt or to taste

5cm (2in) piece of cinnamon stick

2 bay leaves, halved

- Drain the rice and leave it to drain in a colander.

- In a heavy saucepan bring 475ml (16fl oz) water to the boil. Add the remaining ingredients.

- Add the rice and bring back to the boil. Reduce the heat to medium and cook for 4–5 minutes or until the surface water has almost evaporated. Reduce the heat to very low (use a heat diffuser, if necessary, for gentle cooking) and cover the pan tightly. If you do not have a tight-fitting lid, cover with a piece of aluminium foil first, then put the lid on the pan. Cook for 5 minutes.

- Remove from the heat and leave the pan undisturbed for 6–7 minutes. Remove the cinnamon and bay leaves, fluff up the rice with a fork and serve.

SAFFRON RICE

Kesari Chawal

**Preparation time: 5–10 minutes, plus soaking
Cooking time: 10–12 minutes**

Each serving contains
Kcals: 227
g fat: 3.5
g saturated fat: 0.3

Although there are many versions of saffron rice, this recipe is rather special. It derives from the Mogul era and, as well as saffron, it has the irresistible, heady aroma of rose essence. Floral essences were first introduced during the Mogul period and they have been used in Indian cuisine for thousands of years.

225g (8oz) basmati rice, washed and soaked in cold water for 30 minutes

1 tablespoon sunflower or soya oil

4 green cardamom pods, bruised

1 teaspoon royal cumin or caraway seeds

½ teaspoon salt

475ml (16fl oz) warm water

pinch of saffron threads, pounded

4–5 drops of rose essence

a few fresh rose petals, washed and dried, to garnish

- Drain the rice and leave it to drain in a colander.

- In a non-stick saucepan, heat the oil over medium heat. Add the cardamom and royal cumin or caraway seeds and let the spices sizzle for 20–25 seconds.

- Add the rice and fry for 2–3 minutes, stirring.

- Add the salt and pour in the warm water. Bring to the boil and stir in the saffron and rose essence. Reduce the heat to low, cover the pan and cook for 8–10 minutes without lifting the lid. Remove from the heat and leave to stand, undisturbed, for 6–8 minutes.

- With a metal spoon, transfer the rice to a serving dish, surround with the rose petals and serve.

---

* **COOK'S TIP: Concentrated pure rose essence is available in Indian stores, but you could use 1½ tablespoons rose water, which you can buy from large supermarkets.**

FRIED BROWN RICE

SERVES 4

Bhuna hua Chawal

Preparation time: 5 minutes, plus soaking
Cooking time: 15 minutes

Each serving contains
Kcals: 270
g fat: 6
g saturated fat: 0.7

This is the traditional accompaniment for dhansak. Sugar is caramelized in hot oil before the rice is added along with a few whole spices. I find that it tastes just as good with other dishes, such as Lentils with Kidney Beans (see page 132) or Spiced Mixed Lentils (see page 133).

225g (8oz) basmati rice, washed and soaked for 30 minutes

2 tablespoons sunflower oil

4 teaspoons sugar

4 green cardamom pods, bruised

2.5cm (1 in) piece of cinnamon stick

2 cloves

1 bay leaf, crumpled

½ teaspoon salt or to taste

475ml (16fl oz) hot water

- Drain the rice and leave it in a colander to drain.

- In a non-stick saucepan, about 25cm (10in) in diameter, heat the oil over medium heat. When hot, add the sugar and wait until it has caramelized.

- Reduce the heat to low, then add the spices and bay leaf. Let them sizzle for 15–20 seconds, then add the rice and salt. Sauté for 2–3 minutes.

- Pour in the water and bring to the boil. Boil steadily for 2 minutes, then reduce the heat to very low. Cover the pan and cook for 8 minutes.

- Remove the pan from the heat and let it stand for 8–10 minutes undisturbed, without lifting the lid. Fluff up the rice with a fork and serve.

CHICKEN PILAU

Murgh Pulao

Each serving contains
Kcals: 445
g fat: 9
g saturated fat: 2

Preparation time: 20–25 minutes, plus soaking
Cooking time: 25 minutes

The delicate scent and flavour of basmati rice is characteristic of all pilaus. Basmati means fragrant, and this exquisite rice is grown extensively in the foothills of the Himalayas. Northern chefs have stretched their imagination to superlative heights and created an amazing range of recipes for pilau rice. This adaptation of one of these fine recipes, though cooked without using ghee, captures the traditional flavours. It is a real delight to the palate.

280g (10oz) basmati rice

pinch of saffron threads, pounded

2 tablespoons rose water

2 teaspoons white poppy seeds

1 tablespoon sunflower seeds

1–3 dried red chillies, chopped

15–20 black peppercorns

450g (1lb) boneless chicken thighs, skinned and halved

75g (2½oz) low-fat plain yogurt

2 teaspoons Ginger Purée (see page 16)

2 teaspoons Garlic Purée (see page 15)

1 onion, finely sliced

1 tablespoon Ground Roasted Coriander (see page 21)

1 teaspoon Ground Roasted Cumin (see page 20)

5cm (2in) piece of cinnamon stick, halved

6 green cardamom pods, bruised

6 cloves

1½ teaspoons salt or to taste

525ml (18fl oz) Aromatic Stock (see page 23) or hot water

1 tablespoon flaked almonds, toasted

- Wash the rice in several changes of water and soak it for 30 minutes, then leave it in a colander to drain.

- Mix the pounded saffron with the rose water and set aside.

- Using a coffee or spice mill, finely grind the poppy seeds, sunflower seeds, chillies and peppercorns. Set aside.

- In a non-stick saucepan, at least 30cm (12in) in diameter, mix the chicken with the remaining ingredients except the salt, stock or water and flaked almonds. Place the saucepan over high heat and stir until the chicken begins to sizzle. Cook for 6–7 minutes, stirring frequently.

- When the chicken begins to brown, add the ground ingredients, and the salt, then reduce the heat to medium. Continue to cook for a further 2–3 minutes, then stir in the drained rice.

- Pour in the stock or water and bring to the boil, then cover the pan with a piece of aluminium foil and place the lid on top. Reduce the heat to low and cook, without lifting the lid, for 10 minutes.

- Remove the lid and foil, and sprinkle the saffron and rose water mixture randomly on the rice. Discard the foil and cover the pan with the lid, then leave it undisturbed for 8–10 minutes

- Carefully transfer the pilau to a serving dish and garnish with the toasted almonds.

COOK'S TIP: To cook ahead, cook the pilau in advance to the end of step 5. Then complete the cooking just before you are ready to serve the meal.

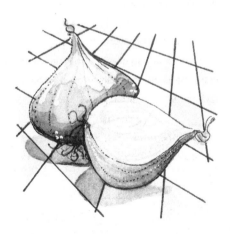

MEATBALLS WITH PILAU RICE

SERVES 4

Kofta Pulao

Each serving contains
Kcals: 415
g fat: 6
g saturated fat: 1.5

**Preparation time: 30 minutes, plus soaking
Cooking time: 30 minutes**

*Traditionally, pulao is a rich dish with ghee, and nuts and raisins are often added.
This version uses traditional spices, but it is cooked with yogurt rather than ghee.*

450g (1lb) minced chicken or turkey

2–3 garlic cloves, peeled and coarsely chopped

2.5cm (1in) cube of fresh root ginger, peeled and coarsely chopped

1–2 green chillies, seeded and chopped

15g (½oz) chopped fresh coriander leaves, including the tender stalks

2 teaspoons ground coriander

1½ teaspoons Garam Masala (see page 22)

55g (2oz) low-fat plain yogurt

1½ teaspoons salt or to taste

1 small onion, coarsely chopped

600ml (1 pint) hot water

4 green cardamom pods

2 x 2.5cm (1in) pieces of cinnamon stick

4 whole cloves

10–12 black peppercorns

2 bay leaves, crumpled

½ teaspoon ground turmeric

280g (10oz) basmati rice, washed and soaked for 30 minutes

15g (½oz) flaked almonds, toasted, to garnish

- Put the chicken in a food processor with the garlic, ginger, chillies, coriander leaves, ground coriander, garam masala, half the yogurt and half the salt. Blend until smooth, then add the onion and process until the onion is fine, but not puréed. Shape the mixture into walnut-sized balls (koftas) – you should have about 28 meatballs.

- Pour the water into a heavy-based saucepan, place over high heat and add the remaining yogurt. Beat with a wire beater until blended, then add the cardamoms, cinnamon, cloves, peppercorns, bay leaves and turmeric.

- Bring to the boil and add the meatballs a few at a time so that the water is kept at boiling point until they are all added. Cover the pan and reduce the heat to low. Simmer for 15 minutes. Stir once or twice after the first 7–8 minutes' cooking, by which time the meatballs will be firm and will not fall apart.

Use a draining spoon to remove the meatballs; set aside and keep hot. Drain the rice and add it to the meat stock with the remaining salt. Increase the heat to high, bring to the boil and boil for 2–3 minutes, then reduce the heat to very low (use a heat diffuser, if necessary, for gentle cooking), cover tightly and cook for 8 minutes.

Pile the koftas on top of the cooked rice and cover the pan. Cook for 2 minutes, then remove from the heat. Leave the pan undisturbed for 8–10 minutes.

Using a flat metal or plastic spoon (a wooden spoon will squash the grains), gently stir the pilau to distribute the koftas. Turn out on to a serving dish and garnish with the toasted almonds. Serve with Spinach Raita (see page 182) and grilled pappadums.

VARIATION: Use lean minced pork or lamb instead of the chicken or turkey.

COOK'S TIP: The meatballs can be made in advance and stored overnight in the refrigerator or frozen. The stock can also be prepared and chilled or frozen. Thaw both before using them in the pilau.

RICH LAMB PILAU

Yakhni Pulao

Each serving contains
Kcals: 540
g fat: 15
g saturated fat: 6.5

Preparation time: 30 minutes, plus soaking
Cooking time: 1¼–1¾ hours

The Mogul Emperors were pampered by their ingenious chefs, who created exotic pilaus and biryanis. A product of the royal kitchens, the word yakhni *means rich meat stock and, in the original version, a large amount of ghee was added when making the stock in which to cook the rice. Ghee is not added to this version and the ingredients have been modified to reduce the fat content, but the result is still a wonderfully aromatic pilau with a lighter, fresher flavour. This pilau is a meal in itself – raita and grilled pappadums are all that is required by way of accompaniments.*

450g (1lb) basmati rice, washed and soaked for 30 minutes

pinch of saffron threads, pounded

2 tablespoons rose water

2 x 5cm (2in) pieces of cinnamon stick, halved

6 green cardamom pods, bruised

6 cloves

1 teaspoon salt or to taste

1 tablespoon flaked almonds, toasted

1-2 tablespoons Browned Sliced Onions (see page 18)

Stock

1 teaspoon black peppercorns

2 tablespoons coriander seeds

2 tablespoons cumin seeds

450g (1lb) lamb neck fillet, cut into 2.5cm (1in) cubes

6 lamb chops or cutlets, trimmed of rind and excess fat

3 x 5cm (2in) pieces of cinnamon stick

8 green cardamom pods, bruised

2 brown cardamom pods, bruised

12 cloves

2 bay leaves

8 garlic cloves, lightly crushed

7.5cm (3in) cube of fresh root ginger, sliced

115g (4oz) low-fat plain yogurt

1 teaspoon salt

- First make the stock. Using a coffee or spice mill, lightly crush the peppercorns, coriander seeds and cumin seeds. You could also do this by putting the spices in a polythene bag and crushing them with a rolling pin. Tie the crushed spices in a piece of muslin cloth (similar to a bought bouquet garni).

- Put both cuts of meat and the spice bag in a large saucepan with all the remaining ingredients for the stock. Pour in 1.2 litres (2 pints) water and bring to the boil. Reduce the heat to low, cover the pan and simmer for 1–1½ hours or until the meat is tender.

- Strain the stock through a sieve. Remove the spice bag, whole spices, bay leaves, ginger and garlic. Hold the spice bag over the stock and squeeze it out to extract all the flavour. Press the garlic and ginger through a sieve into the stock. Mix well and set aside. You should have about 1 litre (1¾ pints); if not, add water to make it up to that amount. Set the meat aside.

- Drain the rice in a colander. Mix the saffron with the rose water and set aside to soak.

- In a non-stick saucepan, about 30cm (12in) in diameter, bring the stock to the boil. Add the cinnamon, cardamoms, cloves, rice and all the reserved cooked meat. Stir in the salt and bring back to the boil.

- Allow to boil for 2 minutes, then reduce the heat to very low (use a heat diffuser, if necessary, for gentle cooking). Cover the pan with a piece of aluminium foil then put the lid on. Cook for 8–10 minutes.

- Sprinkle the saffron and rose water randomly over the pilau. Re-cover and leave to stand for 8–10 minutes.

- To serve, turn out the pilau on to a serving dish and garnish with the toasted almonds and browned onions.

AUBERGINE PILAU

Brinjal Pulao

Preparation time: 15 minutes, plus soaking
Cooking time: 16–17 minutes

Each serving contains
Kcals: 290
g fat: 11
g saturated fat: 1

Aubergines are one of my favourite vegetables. I am always fascinated by the fact that, when cooked, the flesh is transformed into a smooth, velvety texture, absorbing whatever flavour you add to it. This recipe is from the southern coastal area of India where coconut is often used to add a creamy richness. I have used white poppy seeds and sunflower seeds instead, to achieve a similar richness.

225g (8oz) basmati rice, washed and soaked in cold water for 30 minutes

1 medium aubergine, about 280g (10oz)

2 tablespoons sunflower or soya oil

2 x 5cm (2in) pieces of cinnamon stick, halved

4 green cardamom pods, bruised

4 cloves

1 medium onion, finely sliced

½ teaspoon ground turmeric

1 teaspoon salt or to taste

475ml (16fl oz) hot water

Spice mix

2 teaspoons white poppy seeds

2 teaspoons sunflower seeds

2 teaspoons coriander seeds

1–3 dried red chillies, coarsely chopped

½ teaspoon black peppercorns

- First grind the ingredients for the spice mix in a coffee or spice mill.

- Drain the rice and leave it to drain in a colander.

- Quarter the aubergine lengthways. Cut each quarter in half, then into 2.5cm (1in) cubes. Soak the cubes in cold water to prevent them from discolouring, adding salt if you wish, but don't forget to rinse them before cooking.

- In a non-stick saucepan, at least 25cm (10in) in diameter, heat the oil over low heat. Add the cinnamon, cardamoms and cloves and cook gently for 15–20 seconds. Add the onion and increase the heat to medium. Fry for 6–7 minutes, stirring frequently, until the onion is lightly browned.

- Add the ground spice mix and cook, stirring, for 1 minute.

- Drain the aubergine cubes and add them to the pan along with the rice, turmeric and salt. Mix thoroughly and pour in the hot water. Bring to the boil, then reduce the heat and cover the pan tightly. If you don't have a tight-fitting lid, put a sheet of aluminium foil over the pan before putting on the lid. Cook for 10 minutes, then remove from the heat and leave the pilau undisturbed for 10 minutes. Fork through and serve.

---

* **COOK'S TIP: The age-old practice of soaking aubergines in salt or salted water to remove bitterness does not strictly apply to modern aubergines. I rarely follow this method and find no trace of bitterness.**

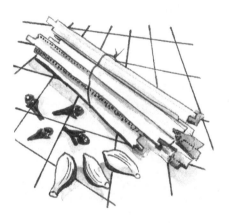

VEGETABLE PILAU

Subzi Pulao

Each serving contains
Kcals: 290
g fat: 6
g saturated fat: 0.75

**Preparation time: 15–20 minutes, plus soaking
Cooking time: 20 minutes, plus standing time**

This is a simple dish with a colourful appearance and fabulous flavours. For a wholesome and tasty vegetarian meal, served it with a lentil dish; it is equally enjoyable with kebabs and a raita.

225g (8oz) basmati rice, washed and soaked in cold water for 30 minutes

2 tablespoons sunflower or soya oil

½ teaspoon cumin seeds

2.5cm (1in) piece of cinnamon stick

4 green cardamom pods, bruised

2 cloves

1 red onion, halved and finely sliced

170g (6oz) carrots, coarsely grated

115g (4oz) fresh spinach, finely shredded
or frozen leaf spinach, thawed and drained

1 teaspoon salt or to taste

½ teaspoon ground turmeric

475ml (16fl oz) warm water

- Drain the rice and leave it to drain in a colander.

- Heat the oil in a non-stick saucepan over medium heat. Add the cumin seeds followed by the cinnamon, cardamoms and cloves. Let the spices sizzle for 15–20 seconds, then add the onion and fry for 4–5 minutes or until the onion has softened.

- Add the carrots and spinach and increase the heat to high. Stir-fry for 2–3 minutes, then reduce the heat to medium and add the rice, salt and turmeric. Fry for 2–3 minutes, stirring constantly, then pour in the warm water.

- Bring to the boil and allow to boil vigorously for 1 minute, then reduce the heat to low. Cover the pan and cook for 10 minutes. Do not lift the lid during this cooking. Remove the pan from the heat without lifting the lid and set it aside to stand, undisturbed, for 5–6 minutes before serving.

CHAPATIS

Chapatis

Each serving contains
Kcals: 95
g fat: 1.5
g saturated fat: 0.2

Preparation time: 10–15 minutes, plus resting
Cooking time: 30 minutes

In an Indian home, chapatis are the equivalent of a loaf of bread in the British household. These everyday breads, made with wholemeal flour, are nutritious and they are a useful source of fibre. This is because the entire wheat kernel is ground into the flour. Oil is not used in traditional recipes, but I find a little oil makes softer chapatis. Warm water, rather than cold water, also helps to give a softer texture.

400g (14oz) chapati flour

1 teaspoon salt

2 tablespoons sunflower or soya oil

250ml (8½fl oz) lukewarm water

- In a large mixing bowl, mix the flour and salt. Add the oil and work it into the flour well, then gradually add the water and mix until a dough is formed. Do not worry if the dough seems a little sticky at first – the excess moisture is absorbed by the flour by the time the dough is ready.

- Transfer the dough to a clean surface and knead it for 4–5 minutes. Alternatively, make the dough in a food processor. Cover the dough with a damp cloth and leave to rest for 30 minutes.

- Divide the dough in half and cut each portion into 8 equal-sized balls. Flatten the balls into round cakes by rotating them between your palms and then pressing them down gently.

- Dust a cake of dough lightly with chapati flour and roll out into a 15cm (6in) disc. Keep the remaining cakes covered with a damp cloth.

- Preheat a heavy cast-iron griddle or other suitable shallow pan over medium-high heat. Place a chapati on it and cook until bubbles begin to appear on the surface. Using a fish slice, turn it over and cook until the underside has brown patches. You can check this by gently lifting the chapati. Turn it over again and press the edges down. The chapati will puff up now. Cook until brown patches appear on the other side. Once the pan is well heated, you may need to turn the heat down slightly.

- Wrap the chapatis in a sheet of aluminium foil lined with kitchen paper to keep hot until you finish cooking all of the dough. Serve with any curry.

---

* **COOK'S TIP:** You can buy wholewheat chapati flour from Indian stores and store it in the same way as ordinary flour. Wholemeal bread flour can be used but it is coarser than atta and I find the chapatis turn out rather dry. A good compromise is to mix wholemeal flour and plain flour in equal quantities.

SPICED CHAPATIS

Masala Chapatis

**Preparation time: 15–20 minutes, plus resting
Cooking time: 30 minutes**

MAKES 16

Each serving contains
Kcals: 95
g fat: 1.5
g saturated fat: 0.2

These chapatis are seasoned with ground cumin and coriander, and chilli powder to pep up their flavour. Chopped coriander leaves add a fresh, zesty flavour to the spiced dough.

400g (14oz) wholewheat chapati flour, plus a little extra for dusting

1 teaspoon salt

1½ teaspoons ground cumin

1½ teaspoons ground coriander

½–1 teaspoon chilli powder

2 tablespoons finely chopped fresh coriander leaves

2 tablespoons sunflower or soya oil

about 250ml (8½fl oz) lukewarm water

- Put the flour in a large bowl and add the remaining ingredients, except the oil and water. Mix well.

- Add the oil and work it well into the flour. Gradually add the lukewarm water – the exact quantity will vary, depending on the absorbency level of the flour you are using. Do not worry if the dough appears a little sticky at first; the flour will absorb all the moisture when you knead it. Transfer the dough to a board and knead it for 4–5 minutes until it is soft and pliable. You can also make the dough in a food processor if you wish. Cover it with a damp cloth and leave to rest for 30 minutes.

- Divide the dough in half and make 8 equal balls out of each piece. Flatten each ball to a smooth round cake by rotating it between your palms. Dust each cake lightly in flour and roll out to a 15cm (6in) disc. While you are working on one, keep the remaining cakes covered with a damp cloth.

- Preheat a heavy cast-iron griddle or other suitable shallow pan over medium-high heat. Place a chapati on it and cook until bubbles begin to appear on the surface. Using a fish slice, turn it over and cook until the underside has brown patches. You can check this by gently lifting the chapati. Turn it over again and press the edges down. The chapati will puff up now. Cook until brown patches appear on the other side. Once the pan is well heated, you may need to turn the heat down slightly.

- Wrap the cooked chapatis in a sheet of aluminium foil lined with kitchen paper to keep hot until you finish cooking all of them. Serve with any curry.

PUFFED GRILLED BREAD

Phulkas

**Preparation time: 10–15 minutes, plus resting
Cooking time: 15–20 minutes**

Each serving contains
Kcals: 75
g fat: 1.2
g saturated fat: 0.2

A phulka is quite similar to a chapati. The same dough is used but it is cooked over an open flame. Traditionally, one side of the phulka is cooked very briefly to leave it undercooked and the other side is cooked fully. Indian housewives have this knack of placing the uncooked side directly on the burning gas, using a pair of tongs. The bread then puffs up beautifully, with a thicker layer at the bottom, a thin layer at the top and a hollow between the two. They are absolutely divine and must be eaten hot. The process of using an open flame needs practice, but do not despair, they can be cooked very successfully under a hot grill. In fact, I find it easier and quicker to use the grill.

1 quantity Chapati Dough (see page 159)

- Divide the dough in half and make 10 equal balls out of each piece. Flatten each ball into a smooth round cake by rotating it between your palms, then pressing down gently. Cover the dough cakes with a damp cloth, then start rolling and cooking the breads one at a time.

- Preheat the grill to high and place a grill pan, without the grid, approximately 12cm (5in) away from the heat source. It is important that the grill pan is also preheated.

- Dust a flattened cake lightly with flour and roll it out to a 12cm (5in) disc. Make sure that the surface of the bread is smooth without any holes or tears, otherwise it will not puff up.

- Preheat a heavy cast-iron griddle or other suitable shallow pan over medium-high heat and place the bread on it. Flip it over after about 20 seconds and allow the other side to cook until brown spots and patches appear. Lift it off gently and place under the grill. The bread will puff up within a few seconds. Wait until light brown patches appear on the surface, then gently remove it from the grill on a spatula. Once the griddle is heated to the right temperature (usually after you have made 2–3 phulkas), you can turn the heat down slightly.

- Wrap the cooked phulkas in a piece of foil lined with absorbent kitchen paper to keep them hot until you have finished making all the breads.

TANDOORI BREAD

Tandoori Roti

Preparation time: 10 minutes, plus proving
Cooking time: 15–20 minutes

Each serving contains
Kcals: 200
g fat: 3
g saturated fat: 0.4

Roti is one of the basic breads baked in the tandoor. The original recipe is unleavened, and nothing other than plain water is used in the dough. It is delicious if you can eat it as it comes out of the oven, but the taste and texture are no longer exciting when the bread is cold, so for this reason I decided to change my recipe. Here is my version, which can be eaten hot or cold. It can also be frozen.

450g (1lb) wholemeal self-raising flour, plus 1–2 tablespoons for dusting

½ teaspoon salt

1 teaspoon sugar

1 sachet easy-blend yeast

1 tablespoon sunflower or soya oil

140g (5oz) low-fat plain yogurt

240–300ml (8½–10fl oz) soda water

- Put the flour, salt, sugar and yeast in a large bowl and mix well.

- Beat the oil and yogurt together and rub into the flour.

- Gradually add the soda water and mix until a dough is formed. Do not worry if the dough feels sticky at this stage; the flour will absorb all the excess moisture when you knead it. Transfer the dough to a board and knead it until it is soft and springy and no longer sticks to the board. You can also make the dough in a food processor if you wish, in which case you should mix the dry ingredients first.

- Put the dough in a large polythene bag and tie it at the top with a twist tie. Place the bag in a warmed bowl and leave the dough to rise in a warm place for 1–1½ hours.

- Preheat the oven to 230°C/450°F/Gas 8. Line a baking sheet with baking parchment or greased greaseproof paper.

- Divide the dough into 8 equal portions. Rotate each portion between your palms to make a smooth round ball, then flatten it to a round cake. Dust it in a little flour and roll it out to a 10cm (4in) disk. Place on the prepared baking sheet and bake on the top shelf of the oven for 9–10 minutes or until puffed and browned in patches.

Side Dishes,
Salads & Relishes

Considering that the majority of the population is vegetarian, it is not surprising that Indian cooks excel in the art of creating imaginative vegetable dishes. Millions of years ago, human beings were vegetarians, living on plants and roots before they developed their hunting skills. Vegetables are still essential for a healthy diet. An Indian diet generally consists of vegetable dishes, small quantities of meat and rice or bread made of wholewheat flour for completely balanced eating.

These days we are extremely lucky to have an endless supply of all kinds of fruits and vegetables from all over the world. I have tried to include a wide range of vegetable recipes that are all quick and easy, as they should be for side dishes. They are simply spiced to enhance, rather than mask, the natural flavours of the main ingredients.

The Indian method of cooking vegetables is very sensible as they are usually cooked slowly in their own juices or their cooking liquid is always used in the sauces. This helps to retain water-soluble vitamins which are otherwise lost in the cooking water when vegetables are boiled and drained. Frozen vegetables have as much nutritional value as fresh. For speed and convenience I have used frozen vegetables in a number of recipes.

When buying vegetables, always make sure that they are as fresh as possible. Avoid any produce that is bruised or beginning to rot in places. If possible, cook fresh vegetables on the day you buy them; if not, wrap them in polythene food bags and store them in the refrigerator.

Salads and relishes are an integral part of any Indian meal. They are not only cooling and an essential balance to the meal, but for the vast majority of the population, who are vegetarians, they are also a great source of protein. Raitas are always yogurt-based and they are sometimes called salads. When making raitas you can use any vegetables or fruits as long as they are absolutely fresh. In most cases I have offered serving suggestions for the salads and raitas, but they can be served with virtually any dish. The chutneys are ideal with snacks and finger foods.

Throughout India, raitas are made in the same way. The regional difference lies only in the spicing and seasoning. For instance, whereas in northern India raitas are flavoured with roasted and ground cumin seeds and chilli powder, in the south they are flavoured with a hot oil seasoning containing mustard seeds, dried chillies and curry leaves.

Yogurt is an excellent source of protein, iron, calcium and thiamine. It is known to assist with gastro-intestinal problems. It is given to invalids and used in weaning babies because it is easily digestible, nutritious and, most importantly, free from harmful organisms.

Indian housewives still make yogurt at home. The yogurt used in India is usually made from buffalo milk, which is creamier than cow's milk. The result is a mild yogurt. Commercial yogurt is set in unglazed earthenware pots, which improves its flavour and texture. Do try and use bio, or live, low-fat yogurt for the recipes in this section – I find it matches Indian yogurt very closely.

SAVOURY POTATO MASH

SERVES 4

Each serving contains
Kcals: 175
g fat: 4.6
g saturated fat: 0.5

Aloo Bharta

Preparation time: 30–35 minutes
Cooking time: 6–8 minutes

Lightly mashed potatoes, seasoned with a hint of spice, are an excellent substitute for traditional Indian staples, such as rice and bread. I have tried serving these with several of the grilled and roasted dishes in this book and, along with the friends who also tasted the dishes, found the combination most enjoyable. The potatoes are equally good with Chapatis (see page 159) and meat or poultry dishes.

675g (1½lb) potatoes, boiled in their skins

1½ tablespoons sunflower or soya oil

½ teaspoon black mustard seeds

½ teaspoon cumin seeds

1–2 green chillies, seeded and finely chopped

1 small red onion, finely chopped, about 2–3 tablespoons

½ teaspoon salt or to taste

¼ teaspoon ground turmeric

2–3 tablespoons finely chopped coriander leaves

- Peel and lightly mash the potatoes to a coarse texture so that there are some whole but small pieces left.

- Heat the oil in a non-stick saucepan over medium heat and add the mustard seeds. As soon as they pop, add the cumin seeds. Add the chillies and onion and fry for 3–4 minutes, stirring frequently. Stir in the salt, turmeric and coriander leaves, then cook for 1 minute.

- Add the potatoes to the pan and stir until the spices and the potatoes are thoroughly mixed and heated through. Serve immediately.

KARNATAKA POTATO CURRY

SERVES 4–6

Each serving contains
Kcals: 200
g fat: 5.3
g saturated fat: 4

Batata Sukkhe

Preparation time: 15–20 minutes
Cooking time: 10–12 minutes

Potatoes are one of nature's most amazing gifts. Not only are they good for us, with their carbohydrate and fibre content, but they also have this quality of absorbing flavours easily. Here is a simple, but fabulous, recipe from the district of Karnataka in the southern coastal region of India. It is a dry spiced dish (the word sukkhe *means dry).*

675g (1½lb) potatoes, cut into 2.5cm (1in) cubes

1 teaspoon salt or to taste

½ teaspoon ground turmeric

1 tablespoon channa dhal or yellow split peas

1–3 dried red chillies, broken up

2 teaspoons coriander seeds

¼ teaspoon fenugreek seeds

30g (1oz) coconut milk powder

150ml (5fl oz) skimmed or semi-skimmed milk, heated

1 tablespoon lemon juice

- Put the potatoes in a large saucepan, about 30cm (12in) in diameter, and add 450ml (15fl oz) water, the salt and turmeric. Bring to the boil, reduce the heat to low and cover the pan. Cook for 6–7 minutes.

- Meanwhile, preheat a small pan over medium heat. Add the channa dhal, chillies, coriander seeds and fenugreek seeds. Reduce the heat to low and stir the mixture for 30–60 seconds or until the spices begin to release their aroma. Transfer the mixture to a plate and allow to cool slightly, then grind to a fine powder in a coffee or spice mill.

- Stir the coconut milk powder into the hot milk and add the ground ingredients. Stir until well blended, then add to the potatoes. Simmer, uncovered, until the potatoes are tender and all the liquid has been absorbed.

- Add the lemon juice and stir gently to mix it into the potatoes without breaking them up. Serve with any bread or as an accompaniment to grilled or baked fish, poultry or meat dishes.

SPICED SWEET POTATOES

SERVES 4

Masaledar Shakurkandi

Preparation time: 10–15 minutes
Cooking time: 15–18 minutes

Each serving contains
Kcals: 200
g fat: 6
g saturated fat: 0.8

Sweet potatoes grow in warm climates, including India. There are many varieties and the type most common in Britain are pink skinned with lovely, moist orange-coloured flesh.

675g (1½lb) sweet potatoes

2 tablespoons sunflower or soya oil

2 teaspoons Garlic Purée (see page 15)

½–1 teaspoon chilli powder

1 teaspoon salt or to taste

½ teaspoon Ground Roasted Cumin (see page 20)

1 teaspoon Ground Roasted Coriander (see page 21)

2 tablespoons finely chopped fresh coriander leaves

- Preheat the oven to 200°C/400°F/Gas 6.

- Peel the sweet potatoes in the same way as ordinary potatoes. Cut them into bite-sized pieces, about 1cm (½in) chunks. Wash and drain the pieces, then dry them thoroughly with a cloth.

- Heat the oil in a roasting tin until it is almost smoking. Add the potatoes, garlic purée, chilli powder and salt. Stir to mix thoroughly, then cook in the oven for 12–15 minutes, stirring two or three times to ensure the potatoes cook evenly.

- Sprinkle the cumin and ground coriander evenly over the potatoes and stir once. Continue to cook for a further 2–3 minutes.

- Stir in the coriander leaves and serve immediately. The sweet potatoes are good with dishes like Chicken in Apricot Juice (see page 70) or Turkey in Orange Juice (see page 95) or with dry dishes, such as Baked Kebabs (see page 104).

---

* COOK'S TIP: When buying sweet potatoes, look for the ones that feel firm and store them with ordinary potatoes, in a cool dry place, away from direct light. Sweet potatoes should not be stored for longer than 7–8 days.

---

* HEALTHY HINT: Sweet potatoes contain fibre, potassium and vitamin C, and they are a rich source of vitamin E. The orange-fleshed variety is a good source of beta-carotene, an antioxidant believed to assist in cancer prevention.

DRY-SPICED OKRA

Bhindi Bhaji

Preparation time: 15–20 minutes
Cooking time: 13–15 minutes

Each serving contains
Kcals: 140
g fat: 10.5
g saturated fat: 1.4

Cultivated in Africa, Egypt and India, okra have beautiful white seeds inside their angular pods. When the vegetables are cut, the sticky seeds tend to make the dish slightly gelatinous, so I prefer to cook okra whole, except when I deep-fry them. Choose small tender okra for this recipe.

250g (9oz) okra

2 small ripe but firm tomatoes, halved and seeded

1 tablespoon sesame seeds

2 tablespoons sunflower seeds

1 tablespoon channa dhal or yellow split peas

1–3 dried red chillies, broken up

1½ tablespoons sunflower or soya oil

½ teaspoon cumin seeds

4–5 fenugreek seeds

1 teaspoon Garlic Purée (see page 15)

½ teaspoon salt or to taste

- Wash the okra thoroughly and slice off the hard stalk end. Cut the tomato halves lengthways into 3–4 pieces.

- Preheat a small pan over medium heat. Add the sesame and sunflower seeds, channa dhal and chillies. Reduce the heat slightly and roast the ingredients, stirring constantly, until the seeds are lightly browned and the dhal or peas have brown spots. Do not allow the seeds to darken. Transfer to a plate and allow to cool slightly, then grind to a smooth powder in a coffee or spice mill.

- Heat the oil in a non-stick pan over low heat. Add the cumin seeds and let them sizzle for 15–20 seconds. Add the fenugreek seeds and garlic purée, and cook for 1 minute, stirring.

- Thoroughly mix in the okra and salt. Cover the pan and cook for 8–10 minutes, stirring occasionally, until the okra is tender, but firm.

- Add the ground ingredients and increase the heat to medium. Stir and cook for 1 minute, then add the tomatoes. Mix well and remove from the heat. Serve with any bread and dishes such as Dry-Fried Lamb (see page 102), Chicken Do-Piaza (see page 80) or Dry-Spiced Chicken Drumsticks (see page 84). For a vegetarian meal, serve with bread or rice, and a lentil or bean dish.

CABBAGE WITH GINGER

Adraki Bandh Gobi

Preparation time: 15 minutes
Cooking time: 20–25 minutes

Each serving contains
Kcals: 88
g fat: 3.5
g saturated fat: 0.5

This side dish can be rustled up in a jiffy and it is good with almost any meal. Ginger is the predominant flavour here – prepare it just before cooking to enjoy its warm, woody aroma which complements the sweet taste of the juicy green cabbage.

1 tablespoon sunflower or soya oil

1cm (½in) cube of fresh root ginger, finely chopped or grated

1 red chilli, seeded and sliced

1 red onion, finely sliced

¼ teaspoon ground turmeric

1 small green cabbage, about 450g (1lb), finely chopped

125g (4½oz) cooked fresh or frozen peas

½–1 teaspoon salt

- Heat the oil in a non-stick saucepan or sauté pan over medium heat and fry the ginger, chilli and onion for 5–6 minutes or until the onion is lightly browned. Reduce the heat slightly halfway through cooking.

- Stir in the turmeric, followed by the cabbage, peas and salt. Mix well, then sprinkle 2 tablespoons water over the vegetables. Reduce the heat to low, cover the pan and cook for 15 minutes, stirring occasionally.

- Cook, uncovered, if necessary, until the vegetables absorb all the cooking juices. Serve immediately.

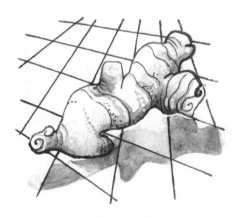

CARROTS AND GREEN BEANS WITH POPPY SEEDS

SERVES 4

Gajjar aur Same

Preparation time: 15 minutes
Cooking time: 20–25 minutes

Each serving contains
Kcals: 92
g fat: 8.7
g saturated fat: 1

This is a quick, tasty and attractive side dish, which can be served with just about any curry and rice or bread. Poppy seeds are generally used to add richness and a nutty flavour, and to thicken sauces. In this recipe, they simply coat the vegetables, making them look and taste delectable.

2 tablespoons white poppy seeds

1 tablespoon sunflower seeds

1 tablespoon sunflower or soya oil

½ teaspoon black mustard seeds

½ teaspoon cumin seeds

1–2 dried red chillies, roughly chopped

2 large garlic cloves, crushed

½ teaspoon ground turmeric

340g (12oz) carrots, cut into 5cm (2in) strips like French fries

340g (12oz) whole green beans, fresh or frozen, cut into 5cm (2in) pieces

½ teaspoon salt or to taste

150ml (5fl oz) warm water

- Preheat a small pan over medium heat. When hot, reduce the heat to low and add the poppy seeds and sunflower seeds. Stir them constantly for 1 minute until they are lightly browned. Do not allow them to darken. Transfer the seeds to a plate to cool, then grind them in a coffee or spice mill and set aside.

- Heat the oil in a non-stick saucepan over medium heat. When hot but not smoking, add the mustard seeds. As soon as they start popping, reduce the heat to low and add the cumin seeds, chillies and garlic. Stir-fry for 1 minute.

- Add the turmeric, followed by the vegetables and salt. Increase the heat to medium and cook for 2 minutes, stirring constantly. Pour in the warm water, cover the pan and reduce the heat slightly. Cook for 15–20 minutes or until the vegetables are tender, stirring occasionally and adding a little more water if necessary. The vegetables should be tender but firm and no water should be left in the pan.

- Add the ground seeds and stir over medium heat for 1 minute. Remove from the heat and serve.

DRY SPICED CARROTS WITH PEAS

SERVES 4

Gajjar aur Matar ki Bhaji

Preparation time: 15 minutes
Cooking time: 15 minutes

Each serving contains
Kcals: 95
g fat: 3.8
g saturated fat: 0.5

Tender and juicy pieces of carrot combine with garden peas to make a delicious side dish in a jiffy. Cut the carrots into small pieces, each no more than double the size of a pea.

250g (9oz) carrots, finely diced

1 tablespoon sunflower or soya oil

½ teaspoon black mustard seeds

½ teaspoon cumin seeds

½ teaspoon black pepper, coarsely crushed

1–2 red chillies, seeded and chopped

250g (9oz) frozen peas

¾ teaspoon salt or to taste

1 tablespoon chopped fresh coriander leaves

1 tablespoon lemon juice

1 tablespoon besan (gram or chick-pea flour)

- Put the carrots in a saucepan and add 300ml (10fl oz) water. Bring to the boil, reduce the heat to medium and cook for 8–10 minutes or until the carrots are tender, but firm. Remove the carrots with a slotted spoon and reserve the cooking water – you should have about 150ml (5fl oz) liquid.

- Heat the oil in a non-stick saucepan over low heat. Add the mustard seeds, then, as soon as they start crackling, add the cumin seeds followed by the pepper and chillies. Cook for 30 seconds.

- Return the carrots to the pan with the peas, salt and reserved cooking liquid. Increase the heat to medium and cook, uncovered, for 5–6 minutes.

- Reduce the heat to low again, then stir in the coriander leaves and lemon juice. Using a fine sieve, sift the besan evenly over the vegetables. Stir until well blended and the vegetables are coated with the besan. Remove from the heat and serve as an accompaniment for any meat or fish curry.

CAULIFLOWER WITH GREEN CHUTNEY

SERVES 4

Hariyali Gobi

Preparation time: 25 minutes
Cooking time: 15–20 minutes

Each serving contains
Kcals: 180
g fat: 10
g saturated fat: 3

Soft green coriander chutney looks quite spectacular on snow-white cauliflower florets and the combination is seriously delicious! The preparation and cooking could not be simpler.

1 large cauliflower

15g (½oz) desiccated coconut

1 small red onion, coarsely chopped

1cm (½in) cube of fresh root ginger, coarsely chopped

2 large garlic cloves, coarsely chopped

15g (½oz) coriander leaves and stalks, coarsely chopped

½ teaspoon salt

1 tablespoon besan (gram or chick-pea flour)

2 tablespoons sunflower or soya oil

2–3 firm but ripe tomatoes, sliced

1–2 red chillies, seeded and cut into julienne strips

- Blanch the cauliflower in salted water for 5 minutes. Drain and refresh in cold water, then cut into 7.5cm (3in) diameter florets. Leave to drain thoroughly in a colander.

- Preheat the oven to 225°C/425°F/Gas 7. Grind the coconut in a coffee grinder or spice mill until fine.

- Put the remaining ingredients, except the tomatoes and chillies, into a blender. Add the coconut and 120ml (4fl oz) water, then blend until smooth.

- Put the cauliflower into a roasting tin and pour over the blended ingredients. Mix thoroughly and cook for 15–20 minutes, or until brown patches appear on the surface of the florets.

- Garnish with the tomatoes and chillies, and serve immediately. The cauliflower complements almost any fish, poultry or meat dish.

---

* **HEALTHY HINT:** Cauliflower provides vitamins C and B6, and folate. It is very low in calories which also makes it ideal for anyone with a weight problem.

MIXED VEGETABLE CURRY

Sabzion ki Kari

Preparation time: 25 minutes
Cooking time: 20 minutes

Each serving contains
Kcals: 200
g fat: 8
g saturated fat: 6

From south India, the characteristic flavours in this simple vegetable curry come from curry leaves and fenugreek seeds. It is good with fish, poultry or meat dishes and it also makes a wholesome vegetarian meal when served with a lentil dish and rice or bread.

2 teaspoons coriander seeds

¼ teaspoon fenugreek seeds

1 tablespoon channa dhal

1–3 dried red chillies, chopped

400g (14oz) potatoes, cut into 2.5cm (1in) cubes

225g (8oz) carrots, cut into 2.5cm (1in) thick slices

¼ teaspoon ground turmeric

¼–½ teaspoon chilli powder

225g (8oz) tomatoes, skinned and chopped
or canned chopped tomatoes, drained

1 teaspoon salt or to taste

125g (4½oz) frozen peas

10–12 fresh or dried curry leaves

40g (1½oz) coconut milk powder

120ml (4fl oz) hot water

- Preheat a small frying pan over medium heat. When hot, reduce the heat to low and add the coriander seeds, fenugreek seeds, channa dhal and chillies. Roast the spices gently for 30–60 seconds, stirring, until they release their aroma. Transfer the spices to a plate and allow to cool, then grind them to a fine powder in a coffee grinder or spice mill.

- Put the potatoes and carrots in a saucepan and add 450ml (15fl oz) water. Bring to the boil and stir in the turmeric and chilli powder. Reduce the heat to low, cover the pan and cook for 5–6 minutes.

- Add the tomatoes and salt, re-cover and cook for 2–3 minutes., then add the peas and curry leaves.

- Whisk the coconut milk powder and hot water together with a wire whisk, making sure there are no lumps, then add to the vegetables with the ground roasted ingredients.

- Bring to a gentle simmer and cook, uncovered, for 6–8 minutes or until the vegetables are tender but firm. Remove from the heat and serve.

SPICED GREEN BEANS

SERVES 4

Each serving contains
Kcals: 60
g fat: 5
g saturated fat: 2.4

Farash Bean Masala

Preparation time: 10–15 minutes
Cooking time: 12–15 minutes

This recipe works very well with either French beans or runner beans. If you use frozen beans, thaw them first, but reserve and use the water released during thawing for maximum nutritional value. This is another versatile side dish with subtle flavours that go with almost any main dish.

250g (9oz) runner beans or green beans

2 teaspoons lemon juice

1 tablespoon sunflower or soya oil

½ teaspoon black mustard seeds

½ teaspoon cumin seeds

¼–½ teaspoon crushed dried red chillies

½ teaspoon salt or to taste

1 tablespoon desiccated coconut

- Trim the runner beans and cut them at a slant into 5mm (¼in) slices. Cut green beans into 2.5cm (1in) pieces.

- Put the beans in a saucepan. Add 300ml (10fl oz) water and the lemon juice (this helps to preserve the fresh colour of the beans). Bring to the boil, then reduce the heat to medium. Cover the pan and cook for 8–10 minutes or until the beans are tender, but still firm.

- Heat the oil in a non-stick saucepan or sauté pan over medium heat. Add the mustard seeds, then, as soon as they pop, add the cumin seeds and the chillies.

- Add the beans to the spices along with the cooking liquid left in the pan. Stir in the salt and coconut, then cook, uncovered, for 3–4 minutes or until most of the liquid has evaporated. The beans should be quite moist and the stock reduced to about 1 tablespoon. Remove from the heat and serve.

---

* **COOK'S TIP: You can buy crushed dried chillies from supermarkets and Indian stores, but it is more economical to grind dried red chillies coarsely in a coffee grinder or spice mill.**

LEEKS WITH COCONUT

Ulli Thoren

Preparation time: 15–20 minutes
Cooking time: 25 minutes

SERVES 4

Each serving contains
Kcals: 108
g fat: 8.6
g saturated fat: 4

This is a quick and easy recipe from Kerala, the exotic spice land in southern India. The traditional recipe uses onions (there is no Indian name for leek, so the Indian title indicates that onions are used), but I have used leeks (or you could use a mixture of red and white onions instead) and added a small quantity of carrots for colour. Curry leaves give most south Indian dishes their distinctive taste. If you do not have fresh or dried curry leaves, add a handful of coriander leaves for a different flavour.

1½ tablespoons sunflower or soya oil

½ teaspoon black mustard seeds

2.5cm (1in) cube of fresh root ginger, peeled and grated

1–2 green chillies, seeded and cut into julienne strips

6–8 curry leaves, fresh or dried

450g (1lb) leeks, halved lengthways and finely sliced

125g (4½oz) carrots, coarsely grated

30g (1oz) desiccated coconut

1 teaspoon salt or to taste

• Heat the oil in a non-stick saucepan over low heat. Add the mustard seeds, then, as soon as they pop, add the ginger, chillies and curry leaves. Cook gently for 1 minute, stirring.

• Add the leeks, carrots, coconut and salt. Stir and sprinkle 3 tablespoons water over the vegetables. Cover the pan and cook for 10 minutes. Add a further 3 tablespoons water, cover and cook for a further 10–12 minutes or until the vegetables are tender. Remove from the heat and serve.

---

* **COOK'S TIP:** Wash leeks thoroughly before cooking. Dirt is often trapped between the layers and the best way of removing it is to wash the leeks under running water when they have been slit lengthways. This rinses out trapped grit.

---

* **HEALTHY HINT:** Leeks contain potassium and folate. Traditional herbalists believe leeks can help as a remedy for sore throat and kidney stones.

FRUIT CURRY

Phalon ki Kari

Each serving contains
Kcals: 315
g fat: 13
g saturated fat: 7

Preparation time: 15–20 minutes
Cooking time: 25–30 minutes

I have adapted this recipe from a hugely popular south-Indian dish in which a selection of fresh and dried fruits are cooked in rich coconut milk extracted from fresh coconut. In this version I have used light coconut milk, which results in a lighter, fresher flavour. To make an exotic meal, serve with Saffron Rice (see page 148).

1 tablespoon sunflower or soya oil

½ teaspoon black mustard seeds

2.5cm (1in) piece of cinnamon stick, halved

1 teaspoon Ginger Purée (see page 16)

½ teaspoon ground cumin

125g (4½oz) fresh pineapple, cut into 2.5cm (1in) cubes

1 teaspoon salt or to taste

85g (3oz) sugar or to taste

½–1 teaspoon chilli powder

150ml (5fl oz) warm water

30g (1oz) unroasted cashew nuts

125g (4½oz) ready-to-eat dried apricots

1 eating apple

1 small, very firm banana

30g (1oz) raisins

45g (1½oz) coconut milk powder blended with 120ml (4fl oz) hot water

1–2 green chillies, seeded and finely chopped

12–15 dried or fresh curry leaves

Garnish

1–2 tablespoons plain fromage frais

about 3 glacé cherries, cut into slivers, rinsed and dried

- Heat the oil in a medium non-stick saucepan over low heat. When hot but not smoking, add the mustard seeds. As soon as they start popping, add the cinnamon stick and ginger purée and fry for 1 minute, stirring.

- Add the cumin and fry for 15–20 seconds, then add the pineapple, salt, sugar and chilli powder. Pour in the warm water, bring to the boil and reduce the heat to medium. Cover and cook for 6–7 minutes.

- Add the cashews and apricots, re-cover and cook for a further 6–8 minutes.

- Meanwhile, peel and core the apple and cut it into 2.5cm (1in) cubes. Cut the banana into thick diagonal slices. Add the apple, banana, raisins and coconut milk to the pan. Bring to a slow simmer and add the chillies and curry leaves. Cook, uncovered, for 8–10 minutes or until all the fruits are tender but still firm.

- Transfer to a serving dish and swirl the fromage frais over the top. Garnish with the cherries and serve.

PINEAPPLE RAITA

SERVES 4

Ananas ka Raita

Preparation time: 15 minutes

Each serving contains
Kcals: 110
g fat: 6.5
g saturated fat: 4

Fresh pineapple is ideal for this raita, but it can be quite sharp in taste unless you can find a fruit that is really ripe and sweet. Supermarkets usually offer two varieties of pineapple: the large cylindrical ones and a smaller round variety with a deeper golden skin. I find the latter is sweeter. It is difficult to be precise about the quantity of sugar needed for fresh pineapple. Drained canned pineapple is a good alternative and it does not need extra sugar when canned in syrup but if using fruit canned in natural juice add sugar to taste.

225g (8oz) mild low-fat plain yogurt

30g (1oz) desiccated coconut, ground to a fine powder in a coffee grinder

½–1 teaspoon salt

caster sugar to taste

½ teaspoon Ground Roasted Cumin (see page 20)

½ teaspoon chilli powder

**225g (8oz) pineapple, fresh or canned,
peeled or drained, as necessary, and cubed**

2 teaspoons sunflower or soya oil

½ teaspoon black mustard seeds

- In a mixing bowl, beat the yogurt with a fork until smooth and stir in the coconut, salt and sugar.

- Reserve a little of the cumin and chilli powder, then add the remainder to the yogurt with the pineapple. Mix well.

- In a small saucepan, heat the oil over medium heat and add the mustard seeds. As soon as they pop, remove from the heat and pour over the raita. Mix well and serve sprinkled with the reserved cumin and chilli powder.

---

* **HEALTHY HINTS: Fresh pineapple is a good source of vitamin C. It is also believed to be a remedy for indigestion, arthritis and catarrh.**

FRUIT RAITA

SERVES 4

Each serving contains
Kcals: 80
g fat: 0.5
g saturated fat: 0.3

Phalon ka Raita

Preparation time: 15 minutes

Raitas are served all over India as a cooling agent and an essential balance to a meal. The regional variation lies only in the flavouring used. In northern India, for example, the favourite way to add zest to a raita is by adding dry-roasted crushed cumin seeds and a little chilli. In this recipe I have used seedless grapes and raisins, a popular combination of the Mogul era, but you can use any ripe fruit you like.

30g (1oz) raisins

140g (5oz) seedless green grapes

1 small ripe pomegranate

170g (6oz) low-fat plain yogurt

½ teaspoon sugar

½ teaspoon salt

½ teaspoon chilli powder

½ teaspoon Ground Roasted Cumin (see page 20)

- Soak the raisins in boiling water for 10 minutes, drain and cool.

- Quarter or halve the grapes according to their size.

- Cut the pomegranate in half. Place one half on a flat surface and hold it, seeds side down, with one hand. Tap all around the shell with the handle of a knife or other similar object (this loosens the seeds and makes it easier to remove them), then remove the seeds by pressing down the shell. Remove any white membrane that is still attached to the seeds. Repeat with the other half.

- In a bowl, beat the yogurt until smooth. Add the sugar, salt, half the chilli powder and half the cumin, and mix well.

- Add the raisins and grapes, and all but 1 tablespoon of the pomegranate seeds. Mix well and transfer the raita to a serving dish.

- Sprinkle the remaining chilli powder and cumin over the raita and garnish with the remaining pomegranate seeds. Serve with any pilau, or with grilled meat, poultry or kebabs.

---

* **HEALTHY HINTS: Grapes and raisins are great energy boosters. They are also rich in vitamins A, B and C as well as potassium. Pomegranate is said to be beneficial to the heart.**

BANANA RAITA

Kela ka Raita

Kcals: 95
g fat: 0.6
g saturated fat: 0.4

Preparation time: 10 minutes, plus chilling

This raita bursts with rich aroma and flavour. Tart lemon juice, sweet raisins and bananas, and the warm, assertive flavour of roasted cumin are perfectly balanced by a hot undertone of chilli. This raita is divine with oily fish, such as mackerel, or rich meat, such as Goan Pork Curry (see page 116) or Baked Kebabs (see page 104). Select ripe bananas that are quite firm, with a hint of green on the skin.

225g (8oz) low-fat plain yogurt

½ teaspoon salt

½ teaspoon Ground Roasted Cumin (see page 20)

½ teaspoon chilli powder

30g (1oz) raisins

2 large ripe, firm bananas

1 tablespoon lemon juice

pinch of coarsely ground black pepper

½ teaspoon paprika

- In a mixing bowl, beat the yogurt with a fork or wire whisk until smooth.

- Add the salt, cumin, chilli powder and raisins. Mix well.

- Peel the bananas and quarter them lengthways. Chop into bite-sized pieces and sprinkle with lemon juice, then mix well. Gently fold the bananas into the yogurt mixture. Cover and chill for 1 hour.

- Transfer to a serving dish, sprinkle with black pepper and paprika and serve.

---

* **HEALTHY HINTS: Bananas have plenty of potassium, which helps muscles and nerves to function efficiently and regulates blood pressure. Their natural sugar content makes them a good source of energy and, in India, bananas are given to babies and adults as a cure for diarrhoea because of their cellulose content.**

BEETROOT RAITA

Chukander ka Raita

Preparation time: 10 minutes

SERVES 4

Each serving contains
Kcals: 60
g fat: 0.5
g saturated fat: 0.3

When mixed with cooked beetroot, plain yogurt goes through a magical transformation in flavour as well as colour. The sweet, slightly earthy taste of beetroot is the perfect match for the slightly tangy yogurt.

225g (8oz) low-fat plain yogurt

½ teaspoon salt

½ teaspoon sugar

1 green chilli, seeded and finely chopped

1 tablespoon fresh coriander leaves, finely chopped

1 teaspoon Ground Roasted Cumin (see page 20)

250g (9oz) cooked beetroot, finely chopped

a few lettuce leaves, finely shredded

- In a mixing bowl, beat the yogurt until smooth and add the salt, sugar, chilli, coriander and half the cumin. Mix thoroughly.

- Stir in the beetroot until thoroughly combined.

- Line a serving dish with shredded lettuce and pile the beetroot raita on top. Sprinkle with the reserved cumin. Serve chilled or at room temperature.

---

* **HEALTHY HINTS: Beetroot is rich in fibre and potassium. In India, beetroot leaves are cooked as a vegetable as they contain essential vitamins and minerals (beta-carotene, calcium and iron).**

SPINACH RAITA

SERVES 4

Palak Raita

Each serving contains
Kcals: 50
g fat: 1
g saturated fat: 0.4

Preparation time: 10 minutes, plus cooling
Cooking time: 8–10 minutes

Flavoured with fresh root ginger and roasted cumin seeds, this makes a delicious side dish. The vitamins and minerals present in spinach combined with the healthy properties attributed to yogurt make up a simple, healthy dish.

250g (9oz) fresh spinach, chopped

2 round slices of fresh root ginger

1 teaspoon cumin seeds

10–12 black peppercorns

225g (8oz) low-fat plain yogurt

½ teaspoon salt

½ teaspoon sugar

- Put the spinach, 120ml (4fl oz) water and ginger in a saucepan and bring to the boil. Reduce the heat slightly and cook, uncovered, for 8–10 minutes or until the water evaporates. Remove from the heat and cool thoroughly.

- Meanwhile, preheat a small heavy-based pan over medium heat and add the cumin seeds and peppercorns. Stir for about 30 seconds or until the spices release their aroma. Transfer to a plate to cool slightly, then crush the spices in a mortar with a pestle.

- Beat the yogurt with a fork until smooth and stir in the salt and sugar. Discard the ginger and add the spinach to the yogurt along with the crushed spices.

- Serve with any curry and rice or bread. This raita is excellent with pilaus and biryanis.

---

* **HEALTHY HINTS: Spinach provides vitamins A, B and C, and potassium. Although spinach contains iron, because it also contains oxalic acid, much of the spinach is unavailable to the body, so it is not a particularly good source of iron in the diet. Research suggests that spinach may be beneficial in preventing certain types of cancer and in treating high blood pressure.**

ALMOND CHUTNEY

Badam ki Chutney

Preparation time: 10 minutes, plus soaking and chilling

Each serving contains
Kcals: 100
g fat: 7
g saturated fat: 0.6

Almonds are highly prized in Indian cooking, especially in the north. Beautiful almond blossoms herald the onset of spring in the northern state of Kashmir, where the nuts grow in abundance. This chutney has a rich, yet refreshing, flavour and can be made in a jiffy; it also keeps well for 5–6 days in an airtight container in the refrigerator.

55g (2 oz) blanched almonds

1 green eating apple, such as Granny Smith

1½ tablespoons lemon juice

2 tablespoons chopped fresh coriander leaves and stalks

12–15 fresh mint leaves

1 green chilli, seeded and chopped

½ teaspoon salt

1 teaspoon sugar

55g (2oz) low-fat plain yogurt

- Put the almonds in a small bowl and add enough boiling water to cover them. Set aside for 15 minutes, then drain.

- Peel, core and coarsely chop the apple. Mix with the lemon juice and put into a blender with the almonds and the remaining ingredients. Blend until smooth.

- Chill the raita for 1 hour before serving as a dip, with any finger food, or as a side dish.

HEALTHY HINTS: Almonds provide protein, iron and potassium. As they are high in calories, only small quantities should be eaten. As well as being a tasty snack, apples are low in fat and calories, and a useful source of vitamin C.

DATE AND RAISIN CHUTNEY

Khajur aur Kishmish ki Chutney

Preparation time: 10 minutes, plus soaking

Each serving contains
Kcals: 85
g fat: 0.11
g saturated fat: 0.02

Unlike its cooked Western counterpart, Indian chutney is made by grinding all the ingredients together to a smooth purée. This chutney is a real treat for its fabulous combination of sweet, savoury, hot and sour accents. It will keep for 2–3 weeks in an airtight jar in the refrigerator.

115g (4oz) stoned dates, chopped

55g (2 oz) raisins

225ml (7½fl oz) boiling water

1¾ teaspoons chilli powder

2¼ teaspoons Ground Roasted Cumin (see page 20)

2 teaspoons tamarind concentrate or 3 tablespoons tamarind juice

2 teaspoons soft brown sugar

1½ teaspoons salt

1 tablespoon low-fat plain yogurt

- Soak the dates and raisins in the boiling water for 30 minutes.

- Reserve ½ teaspoon each of the chilli powder and cumin and place the remainder in a blender. Add the remaining ingredients except the yogurt.

- Add the dates and raisins to the blender with the water in which they were soaked. Blend until smooth.

- Transfer the puréed mixture to a serving dish and swirl the yogurt on top. Sprinkle with the reserved chilli powder and cumin, and serve.

---

* **HEALTHY HINTS: Raisins are a concentrated source of energy and they also contain potassium and iron. Dried dates have a high concentration of potassium.**

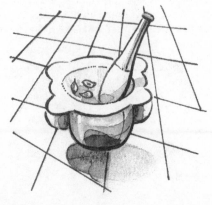

FRESH TOMATO CHUTNEY

Tamatar ki Chutney

Preparation time: 10 minutes, plus cooling
Cooking time: 5–6 minutes

SERVES 4–8

Each serving contains
Kcals: 45
g fat: 2
g saturated fat: 0.25

This tomato chutney is easy to make and it is delicious with all kinds of snacks. It will keep well in the refrigerator in an airtight container for up to 10 days.

340g (12oz) tomatoes, chopped

1 tablespoon sunflower or soya oil

1 onion, chopped

2 large garlic cloves, chopped

2 green chillies, seeded and chopped

2 teaspoons ground cumin

1 teaspoon salt

1 tablespoon sugar or to taste

1 tablespoon finely snipped fresh chives

- Put the tomatoes in a small saucepan. Cook, uncovered, over medium heat for 5–6 minutes or until the tomatoes are soft. Remove from the heat and leave to cool.

- Meanwhile, heat the oil over medium heat and fry the onion and garlic, stirring constantly, for 3–4 minutes.

- Add the chillies and cumin and cook for 30–40 seconds.

- Purée the tomatoes, onion mixture, salt and sugar in a blender or food processor. Transfer to a serving dish, cool thoroughly and stir in the chives.

- Serve chilled.

HEALTHY HINTS: Tomatoes are high in vitamins, particularly beta-carotene from which vitamin A is generated, and potassium. Research suggests that antioxidants present in tomatoes help to reduce the risk of cancer and heart disease.

FRESH VEGETABLE PICKLE

Achar Subz

MAKES 450g (1lb)

Each serving contains
Kcals: 8
g fat: 0.15
g saturated fat: 0.02

Preparation time: 15–20 minutes
Cooking time: 10 minutes

This pickle is very similar to piccalilli which originated in colonial India. This is a south Indian version, in which lemon or lime juice is used instead of vinegar. Serve with any tandoori dishes, grilled or baked meat, poultry and fish. My favourite is a bowl of freshly cooked basmati rice, cold tandoori chicken and this pickle. The pickle can be served straight away, but it tastes better if it is allowed to mature for at least 24 hours. You can store it in the refrigerator for up to 2 weeks.

2 teaspoons salt

1 teaspoon sugar

1cm (½in) cube of fresh root ginger, peeled and grated

1–2 green chillies, seeded and finely chopped

½ teaspoon ground turmeric

½ teaspoon asafoetida

¼–½ teaspoon chilli powder

1 tablespoon cornflour

2 teaspoons made English mustard

2 tablespoons lemon juice

170g (6oz) cauliflower, cut into very small florets, about 3mm (⅛in)

170g (6oz) carrots, very finely chopped

125g (4½oz) fine green beans, finely chopped

- Put the salt and sugar in a medium saucepan and add 240ml (8fl oz) water. Bring to the boil, then boil for 5 minutes.

- Reduce the heat to low and stir in the ginger, green chillies, turmeric, asafoetida and chilli powder.

- Blend the cornflour to a smooth paste with a little cold water and add to the pan with the mustard. Cook, stirring, until the sauce has thickened, then add the lemon juice, and remove from the heat.

- Put the vegetables in a heatproof bowl and add the sauce. Mix and cool.

- Leave the pickle at room temperature for 24 hours, then transfer to an airtight container and chill until required.

* **HEALTHY HINT: Asafoetida has digestive and disinfectant properties. In Indian cooking it is used in those difficult-to-digest dishes, such as deep-fried snacks, and dishes containing lentils or pulses.**

CABBAGE SALAD

SERVES 4

Bandhgobi Salat

Preparation time: 10–15 minutes, plus chilling

Each serving contains
Kcals: 52
g fat: 2.7
g saturated fat: 8

White cabbage is best for this salad. The heart of a green cabbage, especially spring cabbage, can also be used, but remove most of the outer leaves.

15g (½oz) desiccated coconut

25ml (1fl oz) hot water

280g (10oz) white cabbage, finely shredded

1 green chilli, seeded and finely chopped

1 small red onion, finely chopped

1 tablespoon finely chopped fresh coriander leaves

1 tablespoon lemon juice

½ teaspoon salt or to taste

4–6 cherry tomatoes, halved

- In a small bowl, mix the coconut with the hot water and set aside for 10 minutes.

- In a large mixing bowl, mix the remaining ingredients, except the salt and cherry tomatoes. Add the coconut (with any liquid) and mix well. Cover the bowl and chill for 1 hour.

- Stir in the salt and transfer the salad to a serving dish. Garnish with the cherry tomatoes and serve.

---

* **HEALTHY HINTS: Cabbage is high in vitamins and low in calories. Raw cabbage is an excellent source of vitamin C. It also contains beta-carotene, fibre, calcium and potassium.**

CUCUMBER AND PEANUT SALAD

SERVES 4

Kamang Kakdi

Preparation time: 10–15 minutes

Each serving contains
Kcals: 130
g fat: 11
g saturated fat: 5

This is a recipe from the simple, but exciting and extensive, repertoire of the Saraswat community in the Karnataka district of southern India. The cool, crisp cucumber, hot undertone of the green chilli, sweetness of coconut and tartness of lime juice is superlative, and roasted peanuts add crunchiness.

2 tablespoons desiccated coconut

55g (2oz) roasted peanuts

350g (12¼oz) cucumber, finely chopped

1½ tablespoons lime juice

1 tablespoon very finely chopped fresh coriander leaves

1 green chilli, seeded and finely chopped

½ teaspoon salt or to taste

½ teaspoon sugar

- Grind the coconut in a spice or coffee mill to a smooth powder. Coarsely crush the peanuts.

- Mix all the ingredients together and serve.

---

* COOK'S TIP: The salad can be prepared in advance, but do not add the peanuts, salt and sugar until just before serving.

KOHLRABI SALAD

Kohlrabi Salat

Preparation time: 10–15 minutes, plus cooling
Cooking time: 7–8 minutes

SERVES 4

Each serving contains
Kcals: 99
g fat: 4.6
g saturated fat: 3.5

If you have never cooked or eaten kohlrabi before, this is the recipe to try. It is easy to cook, delicious and healthy. You can buy kohlrabi from all good supermarkets: peel and cut it just like a turnip.

1 kohlrabi, about 250g (9oz)

2 carrots, about 170g (6oz), cut into 5mm (¼in) dice

1cm (½in) cube of fresh root ginger, peeled and grated

1 green chilli, seeded and finely chopped

½ teaspoon salt

½ teaspoon sugar

30g (1oz) desiccated coconut

225g (8oz) low-fat plain yogurt

½ teaspoon Ground Roasted Cumin (see page 20)

½ teaspoon chilli powder or paprika

shredded lettuce leaves to serve

Slice off both ends of the kohlrabi, peel and cut into 5mm (¼in) cubes. Place in a saucepan.

Add the carrots, ginger and 150ml (5fl oz) water. Bring to the boil, reduce the heat to medium, cover the pan and cook for 3–4 minutes. Remove the lid and continue to cook for 4–5 minutes. The vegetables should be al dente, tender but with bite.

Remove the vegetables with a slotted spoon and set aside. Boil the cooking water until it is reduced to half its original volume. Stir in the chopped green chilli, salt and sugar and remove from the heat. Leave to cool.

Meanwhile, grind the coconut in a coffee grinder or spice mill to a smooth powder. Stir the coconut into the cooled liquid and transfer to a mixing bowl. Add the yogurt and whisk until smooth.

Add half the cumin and the cooked vegetables. Mix well and transfer to a serving dish. Serve chilled or at room temperature, sprinkled with the remaining cumin and chilli powder or paprika, and surrounded by shredded lettuce.

HEALTHY HINTS: Kohlrabi is rich in potassium and vitamin C. It is also a source of both soluble and insoluble fibre (the former is believed to be helpful in lowering blood cholesterol).

Desserts

The custom of serving dessert is not common in India, where sweet specialities are served only on festive occasions, such as at weddings. Dairy products are the main ingredients for traditional Indian desserts, which combine alluring colours, flavours and textures, and most are delicately scented with rose or kewra (screwpine) essences. On a daily basis, fruit is usually eaten after a meal, which is not only healthier, but also refreshing after spicy food.

Most Indian restaurants in Britain tend to serve sweetmeats instead of traditional desserts. Indian sweetmeats are very sweet and, authentically, they are eaten with tea instead of biscuits or cakes.

I have developed a few dessert recipes based on fruit, one of nature's greatest gifts. Low-calorie fruit is vital in a healthy diet, providing vitamin C and other valuable antioxidants. Many types also provide plenty of fibre. The recipes that follow suit the principles of healthy eating and are quick and easy to make – in fact, they are perfect to round off a spicy meal.

MELON AND MANGO DESSERT

SERVES 4–5

Tarbooz aur Aam ka Mitha

Preparation time: 15–20 minutes

Each serving contains
Kcals: 140
g fat: 0.88
g saturated fat: 0.33

Mango is India's most cherished fruit. The season is short and when it starts there is a certain euphoria among traders and consumers alike. Indian mangoes are not sold in British supermarkets, but there is a regular stock of other varieties. Indian shops sell mangoes imported from India from May to July. Mango and watermelon is a stunning combination in this simple dessert which is cooling and delicious, and looks rather spectacular.

1 watermelon

400g (14oz) sweetened mango purée

¼ teaspoon grated nutmeg

½ teaspoon ground cinnamon

½ teaspoon ground ginger

1–2 tablespoons caster sugar

a few fresh mint leaves to decorate

- Cut the melon in half, remove the seeds and scoop out the flesh with a melon baller, discarding the seeds in the flesh as you work.

- Mix the mango purée with the nutmeg, cinnamon and ginger. Taste, then add the sugar if necessary. Pour it into a shallow serving dish and arrange the melon balls on top. Decorate with the mint leaves and chill for several hours.

---

* **COOK'S TIP:** In this recipe I have used mango purée which is sold in Indian shops, I like to use Indian mango purée because it is made of a special variety of fruit known as 'Alphonso'. It has a rich yellow colour and a distinctive flavour. Alternatively, purée drained canned or prepared fresh mango in a blender or food processor and sweeten the purée to taste with caster sugar.

MANGO DESSERT

Aam ka Mitha

Preparation time: 10–15 minutes, plus soaking and chilling

Each serving contains
Kcals: 300
g fat: 19
g saturated fat: 11

This delectable dessert is deceptively easy to prepare. Buy ready-to-use mango purée from Indian stores or purée drained canned mango and sweeten it to taste.

40g (1½oz) unroasted cashew nut pieces

30g (1oz) raisins

½ teaspoon saffron threads, pounded

75ml (2½fl oz) skimmed or semi-skimmed milk

1 ripe fresh mango

450g (1lb) sweetened mango purée

150ml (5fl oz) double cream substitute

1 tablespoon cornflour

150ml (5fl oz) low-fat fromage frais

¼ teaspoon nutmeg

- Put the cashews and raisins in a bowl. Place the saffron in a small saucepan and add the milk. Bring to the boil, then pour the saffron-infused milk over the cashews and raisins. Cover and set aside for 15–20 minutes.

- Carefully peel the mango with a sharp knife and slice off the flesh from either side of the central, large, flat stone, then remove the two thinner slices on the ends. Use a sawing action when cutting to avoid squashing the flesh, which is smooth, silky and quite delicate. Cut the slices lengthways into thin slithers and set aside.

- Mix the mango purée with the cream substitute in a saucepan. Blend the cornflour to a smooth paste with a little water, then stir it into the mango mixture. Stir over low heat until thickened, but do not allow the mixture to boil. Remove from the heat and stir in the fromage frais, saffron-flavoured milk and most of the fresh fruit, reserving some for decorating the dessert. Allow to cool completely.

- Transfer the cooled mango mixture to a serving dish or individual stemmed glasses. Decorate with the reserved mango and chill for several hours. Sprinkle with nutmeg and serve.

---

* **HEALTHY HINT: Mango is easy to digest and it is rich in beta-carotene and vitamin C, both antioxidants that are great boosters to the body's defence mechanism.**

PAPAYA DESSERT

SERVES 4

Papita ka Mitha

Each serving contains
Kcals: 150
g fat: 0.5
g saturated fat: 0.13

Preparation time: 20 minutes, plus cooling and chilling
Cooking time: 5 minutes

Sweet and succulent golden papaya on raspberry-red sauce, decorated with emerald-green mint, looks absolutely spectacular and let me assure you that this dessert tastes every bit as good as it looks.

500g (1lb 2oz) raspberries

5cm (2in) piece of cinnamon stick, halved

75–125g (2½–4½oz) light soft brown sugar

1½ tablespoons arrowroot

1 tablespoon brandy (optional)

2 large ripe papaya

a few fresh mint leaves to decorate

- Purée the raspberries in a blender and press the purée through a sieve into a saucepan. Add the cinnamon and sugar, then place over low heat. Bring to simmering point, but do not boil.

- Blend the arrowroot to a smooth paste with a little cold water and stir into the fruit purée. Cook gently, stirring all the time, until the sauce thickens. Remove from the heat and set aside to cool, then stir in the brandy (if using).

- Meanwhile, halve the papaya lengthways and remove the seeds. Scrape off the white membrane next to the flesh. It is easier to do this with a grapefruit spoon, which has a serrated edge. Peel the papaya and cut it into bite-sized pieces, then pile them on a serving dish.

- Remove the cinnamon from the sauce then drizzle some of the sauce over the papaya. Pour some sauce around the edge of the fruit to form a border.

- Chill the dessert and remaining sauce for several hours before serving, offering the remaining sauce separately. Decorate with mint leaves.

---

* COOK'S TIP: Papaya seeds have a peppery taste. They can be dried and used along with one or two other whole spices, such as cumin and mustard seeds, as a seasoning cooked in hot oil for vegetables and lentils.

PINEAPPLE AND FIG DESSERT

SERVES 4–5

Ananas aur Anjeer ka Mitha

Each serving contains
Kcals: 130
g fat: 0.4
g saturated fat: 0.05

Preparation time: 20 minutes, plus cooling and chilling
Cooking time: 10–12 minutes

Fresh sweet pineapple is heavenly flavoured with star anise and cinnamon. Look for golden-skinned, ripe pineapple, which will taste sweet: if you cannot find really sweet fruit, adjust the quantity of sugar to taste. Fresh figs make this dessert look exotic, but other fruits can be used, such as kiwi and/or large strawberries cut into quarters. Dried figs can also be used.

1 large extra-sweet pineapple

55–85g (2–3oz) dark soft brown sugar

2 star anise

5cm (2in) piece of cinnamon stick, halved

2 teaspoons arrowroot

1 tablespoon crème de menthe or a few fresh mint leaves

4 fresh figs, quartered

- Quarter the pineapple lengthways and peel it with a sharp knife. Use a small, sharp knife to remove the spines or eyes. Cut the flesh into bite-sized pieces and place them in a serving dish.

- Put the sugar, star anise and cinnamon in a small saucepan and add 300ml (10fl oz) water. Bring to the boil and reduce the heat to low. Continue to cook, uncovered, for 8–10 minutes.

- Blend the arrowroot with a little water and stir it into the syrup. Cook, stirring, until the syrup has thickened slightly. Remove the cinnamon and pour the hot syrup over the pineapple. Place the star anise on top and set aside to cool, then chill for several hours.

- Just before serving the dessert, sprinkle the crème de menthe over the pineapple or decorate with the mint leaves, then arrange the figs on top.

---

* **COOK'S TIP:** For convenience, use canned pineapple in natural juice.

---

* **HEALTHY HINT:** Fresh pineapple is a good source of vitamin C. Figs, both fresh and dry, provide calcium, iron and potassium as well as fibre.

PRUNE AND BANANA DESSERT

SERVES 4

Alubukhara aur Keley ka Mitha

Each serving contains
Kcals: 240
g fat: 7
g saturated fat: 2.5

Preparation time: 15 minutes
Cooking time: 15–20 minutes

Dried prunes and bananas are a healthy combination in this quick-and-easy dessert, which can be served on its own or with low-fat fromage frais drizzled with runny honey.

4 firm, ripe bananas, thickly sliced

1 tablespoon coconut

125g (4½oz) stoned ready-to-eat dried prunes

finely grated rind and juice of 1 lime

juice of 1 orange

1 star anise

30g (1oz) dark soft brown sugar

30g (1oz) pecan nuts or walnut halves

1 tablespoon brandy or dark rum (optional)

- Preheat the oven to 160°C/325°F/Gas 3.

- Put the bananas in an ovenproof dish and sprinkle the coconut over them. Add the prunes, followed by the lime rind and juice, and orange juice. Mix gently with a metal spoon and bury the star anise under the bananas in the centre of the dish.

- Sprinkle the sugar over the fruit and arrange the nuts on top. Cook for 15–20 minutes.

- Remove from the oven and allow to cool for 10–12 minutes, then gently stir in the brandy or rum (if using). Serve at room temperature.

---

* **HEALTHY HINT: Bananas are easily digested and a good source of potassium. Prunes also provide potassium as well as fibre and iron. Prunes are well-known as a cure for constipation.**

SPICED PEARS

Masaledar Nashpati

Preparation time: 10 minutes
Cooking time: 20 minutes, plus chilling

Each serving contains
Kcals: 200
g fat: 3
g saturated fat: 1.8

Serve these lightly spiced pears poached in cider for a refreshing finish to a spicy meal. Rooh afza, a concentrated rose-flavoured syrup, is mixed with plain fromage frais to serve with the pears. Although you will need to make a trip to an Indian store to buy it, once you have rooh afza, you will find all sorts of different uses for it – it is great for flavouring ice-cream, crème fraîche, milk shakes and yogurt. Rooh afza is also known as the summer drink of the east: to make a non-alcoholic drink, simply dilute it to taste and serve in tall glasses over crushed ice.

6 firm William pears

600ml (1 pint) dry cider

7.5cm (3in) piece of cinnamon stick, halved

2 star anise

4 tablespoons sugar

250ml (8½fl oz) low-fat fromage frais

2 tablespoons *rooh afza* or 3 tablespoons rose-flavoured syrup

a few crystallized rose petals, to decorate (optional)

- Peel, quarter and core the pears. Put them in a saucepan and add the remaining ingredients, except the fromage frais and *rooh afza*. Cover and simmer gently until the pears are al dente (tender but firm).

- Use a draining spoon to transfer the pears to a dish. Strain the syrup into a small saucepan and boil until it is reduced to about 3 tablespoons. Spoon it over the pears and allow to cool, then chill for 2 hours.

- Mix the fromage frais and *rooh afza* together and spoon into a small serving dish so that diners can help themselves.

- Arrange the pears in individual serving dishes and decorate with rose petals if wished.

---

* COOK'S TIP: To make crystallized rose petals, choose a rose in your favourite colour and remove a few petals. Wash and dry the petals, then place them on a sheet of greaseproof paper and brush them lightly with beaten egg white. Sprinkle caster sugar on them and leave to dry completely. If you are worried about using raw egg, use the rose petals without crystallizing. They will look just as attractive.

---

* HEALTHY HINT: Pears are among the types of food which are not likely to cause allergic reactions.

ROSE-FLAVOURED ICED DESSERT

SERVES 6–8

Gulab ki Kulfi

Each serving contains
Kcals: 330
g fat: 21.5
g saturated fat: 13

Preparation time: 5 minutes, plus cooling and freezing
Cooking time: 12–15 minutes

Kulfi was introduced to the Indian cuisine by the Moguls. This frozen dessert has a denser texture than the average ice-cream and it is set in small conical-shaped metal moulds. Traditionally, full-cream milk is simmered gently until it is reduced by half, but I have used semi-skimmed milk with low-fat evaporated milk and a substitute for double cream instead. Rose-flavoured syrup is sold by Indian grocers and it adds an exotic scent as well as colour to the dessert.

300ml (10fl oz) semi-skimmed milk

400g (14oz) can reduced-fat evaporated milk

300ml (10fl oz) double cream substitute

75–125g (3½–4½oz) caster sugar

2–3 tablespoons *rooh afza* or rose-flavoured syrup

a few fresh rose petals to decorate

- Lightly grease a heavy non-stick saucepan (this will prevent the milk from sticking to the pan) and pour in the milk, evaporated milk and cream substitute. Add the sugar and bring to the boil over medium heat, stirring frequently.

- Reduce the heat to low and continue to cook for 8–10 minutes, stirring regularly. Remove from the heat and stir in the *rooh afza* or rose-flavoured syrup. Allow to cool, stirring occasionally to prevent a skin from forming on top.

- Pour the mixture into six to eight moulds and freeze for 5–6 hours or until firm.

- To unmould the desserts, hold a mould upside-down under cold running water for 20–25 seconds, taking care not to allow water into the frozen mixture. Quickly dry the outside of the mould with a tea-towel and hold it between the palms of your hands for a few seconds. Then invert the mould on to a plate and lift it off the kulfi. Repeat with the remaining desserts.

- Decorate the desserts with rose petals. Serve the kulfi on its own or offer half portions with fresh fruit to reduce the overall fat content of the dessert.

---

* **COOK'S TIP: Conical kulfi moulds are available in plastic as well as metal from Indian stores. Alternatively, ice lolly moulds can be used.**

YOGURT DESSERT

SERVES 4–5

Shrikand

Preparation time: 10 minutes, plus draining and chilling

Each serving contains
Kcals: 274
g fat: 19.6
g saturated fat: 11.2

Shrikand originated in the state of Maharashtra in western India, of which Bombay is the capital. It is one of the easiest, simplest and most delicious desserts you can make. The yogurt is drained through muslin for several hours by which time it has a consistency similar to cream cheese. Although Greek yogurt is strained, it contains some water which has to be removed. Traditionally, the dessert is flavoured with saffron and cardamom, but I like to use saffron and rose water or rose essence.

2 x 425g (15oz) cartons Greek strained yogurt

pinch of saffron threads, pounded

2 tablespoons hot milk

30–55g (1–2oz) caster sugar or to taste

3–4 drops of rose essence or 2 tablespoons rose water

To serve

fresh fruit, such as blueberries, red currants, kiwi fruit and strawberries

- Line a bowl with a large square of muslin or fine cotton cloth and spoon the yogurt into it. Bring the corners together and tie them so that the yogurt is held in the middle.

- Put the cloth containing the yogurt into a sieve or colander over a bowl and chill for 2–3 hours or until the whey is removed. (Seasoned with a little salt and pepper or sweetened to taste and chilled, the whey makes a delicious and healthy drink.)

- Soak the saffron in the hot milk for 20 minutes. Turn the strained yogurt out of the cloth into a large mixing bowl. Add the saffron and beat the yogurt until smooth.

- Add the sugar and rose essence or rose water, mix thoroughly and chill for several hours.

- Serve the dessert in individual stemmed glasses and decorate with fresh fruit.

---

* **HEALTHY HINT: For a lower-fat version of this traditional dessert, use fat-free Greek strained yogurt and serve with plenty of fresh fruit.**

INDEX

172
fresh vegetable pickle, 186
channa dhal, 10
  lentils with kidney beans, 132
  minced lamb kebabs, 37–8
chapati flour, 5
  wholewheat chapati flour, 10
chapatis, 159
  spiced chapatis, 160
cheese, 3, 8
  chick peas with Indian cheese, 129
  cottage cheese canapés, 43
  Indian cheese kebabs, 40–1
chick-pea flour, 8
chick peas:
  chick peas in tomato sauce, 128
  chick peas with Indian cheese, 129
  stuffed peppers, 46
chicken, 65–95
  aromatic stock, 23–4
  baked chicken, 90–1
  chicken do-piaza, 80–1
  chicken in apricot juice, 70–1
  chicken in coconut milk, 72–3
  chicken in green sauce, 85
  chicken in lentil sauce, 78–9
  chicken in milk, 68–9
  chicken in tomato and coconut sauce, 88
  chicken in yogurt, 67
  chicken korma, 76–7
  chicken meatballs in a rich sauce, 86–7
  chicken pilau, 150–1
  chicken tikka, 34
  chicken tikka masala, 89
  chicken with chilli and lime, 74–5
  chilli chicken, 82–3
  dry-spiced chicken drumsticks, 84
  fat content, 3
  meatballs with pilau rice, 152–3
  semi-tandoori chicken, 94
  silky chicken kebabs, 35–6
  spicy roast chicken, 92–3
  tandoori chicken, 32–3

chillies, 6
  chicken with chilli and lime, 74–5
  chilli chicken, 82–3
  fish in coconut milk, 55
  Goan pork curry, 116–17
  minced lamb kebabs, 37–8
  pork vindaloo, 118–19
  silky chicken kebabs, 35–6
  spiced mixed lentils, 133
  steamed pork balls, 42
cholesterol, 1
choley-paneer, 129
chukander ka raita, 181
chutneys, 183–85
  almond chutney, 183
  cauliflower with green chutney, 172
  date and raisin chutney, 184
  fresh tomato chutney, 185
cider:
  Goan pork curry, 116–17
  pork vindaloo, 118–19
  spiced pears, 198
cinnamon, 6
  cinnamon rice, 147
  garam masala, 22
cloves, 6
  garam masala, 22
coconut, 3, 6–7
  chicken in tomato and coconut sauce, 88
  leeks with coconut, 175
coconut milk, 6–7
  chicken in coconut milk, 72–3
  fish in coconut and coriander sauce, 57
  fish in coconut milk, 55
  fish in tamarind juice, 60
  fruit curry, 176–7
  lamb in coconut milk, 108–9
cod:
  baked fish, 52
  fish in mustard sauce, 56
cooking techniques, 3
coriander leaves, 7
  almond chutney, 183
  chicken in green sauce, 85

steamed semolina cakes with
spicy lentils, 130–1
trout:
tandoori-style fish, 61–2
turkey:
meatballs with pilau rice, 152–3
turkey in orange juice, 95
turkey narangi, 95
turmeric, 9

ulli thoren, 175

vegetables:
fresh vegetable pickle, 186
mixed vegetable curry, 173
side dishes, 163–77
vegetable korma, 136–7
vegetable pilau, 158
vegetable soup, 27
vegetarian main meals, 125–42
vindaloo, pork, 118–19

watermelon:
melon and mango dessert, 193
mung bean and watermelon
curry, 138
weight loss, 4

wholewheat chapati flour, 10

yakhni pulao, 154–5
yellow split peas, 10
lentils with kidney beans, 132
yogurt, 3, 10, 164
almond chutney, 183
banana raita, 180
beetroot raita, 181
chicken in apricot juice, 70–1
chicken in yogurt, 67
chicken korma, 76–7
chicken tikka, 34
fish tikka, 28–9
fruit raita, 179
kohlrabi salad, 189
marinated leg of lamb, 106–7
minced lamb kebabs, 37–8
pancakes with spicy potato filling,
134–5
pineapple raita, 178
semi-tandoori chicken, 94
spinach raita, 182
steamed semolina cakes with
spicy lentils, 130–1
yogurt dessert, 200

LIST OF SUPPLIERS:

AVON

Barts Spices Ltd
York Road
Bedminster
Bristol BS3 4AD
Tel: 0117 977 3474
Fax: 0117 972 0216

EDINBURGH

Nastiuks (Wholesaler)
1 Garden Field
Nine Mile Burn
A702 South of Edinburgh
Midlothian EH26 9LT
Tel: 01986 679 333

GLASGOW

Oriental Food Stores
303-5 Great Western Road
Glasgow G4 9HS
Tel: 0141 334 8133

HUMBERSIDE

Indian and Continental Food Stores
69 Prince's Avenue
Hull HU5 3QN
Tel: 01482 346 915

LONDON

Patel Bros
187-9 Upper Tooting Road
London SW17 7TG
Tel: 020 8767 6338

Dadu's Ltd
190-8 Upper Tooting Road
London SW17 7EW
Tel: 020 8672 4984

Asian Food Centre
540-544 Harrow Road
Maida Vale
London W9 3GG
Tel: 020 8960 3731

MIDDLESEX

Asian Food Centre
175-7 Staines Road
Hounslow
Middlesex TW3 3JB
Tel: 020 8570 7346

SURREY

Spicyfoods Cash and Carry
460 London Road
Croydon
Surrey CR0 2SS
Tel: 020 8684 9844

Atif's Superstore
103 Walton Road
Woking
Surrey GU21 5DW
Tel: 01483 762 774

YORKSHIRE

Bhullar Bros Ltd
44 Springwood Street
Huddersfield
West Yorkshire HD1 4BE
Tel: 01484 531 607

MAIL ORDER

Fox's Spices
Unit J & K
Mason's Road Industrial Estate
Stratford-upon-Avon
Warwickshire CV37 9NF
Tel: 01789 266 420
Fax: 01789 267 737

Natco Spices
T Choithram and Sons (Stores) Ltd
Choithram House
Lancelot Road
Wembley
Middlesex HA0 2BG
Tel: 020 8903 8311
Fax: 020 8900 1426

ONLINE

www.exoticspice.co.uk